UNDER HIS WINGS

What I Learned from God while Watching Birds

Joy DeKok
and Cristine Bolley

BARBOUR BOOKS
An Imprint of Barbour Publishing, Inc.

UNDER HIS WINGS

Published by Barbour Books, an imprint of Barbour Publishing, Inc., P.O. Box 719, Uhrichsville, OH 44683
www.barbourbooks.com

Member of the
Evangelical Christian
Publishers Association

Printed in the United States of America.

Dedicated to

Joy's parents, Ruth and Clarence Pater,
who encouraged her love for the birds
and her desire to learn about them.
And to the memory of
Cristine's grandparents,
Irving and Ruth Woodbury,
who taught their family to feed the birds.

"Are not five sparrows
sold for two pennies?
And [yet] not one of them
is forgotten or uncared for
in the presence of God."

LUKE 12:6 AMPLIFIED

Contents

A Note from Cristine

My grandfather fed the birds that wintered at his Kansas farm. Every fall, he bought a truckload of birdseed and stored it in one of the rooms of his barn. I followed his footsteps through the deep snow to get more seed for the feeders as he explained, "I fill nine bird feeders three times a day through the winter months."

Even as a child, I understood that was a lot of birdseed. Grandpa was a man of few words who spoke through twinkling eyes that watered when it was time for us to leave. In the summer, I spent long hours following this man around the farm. We rode on the tractor together, I watched him make shelves in his workshop, and I picked cherries beside him in the orchard. I only remember a few times that he actually talked to me, once to say he had seen a deer in a field, another to point out he hadn't received any letters from me, and then this passing comment about filling the feeders.

He opened the door to the grain bin, picked up a deep shovel that leaned against the wall, and with two easy sweeps, he filled a large bucket sitting near the mound of seed that towered above my head. I watched him fill the feeders from inside the house, because I was already numbed by the January freeze. A variety of birds patiently waited in the cedars around Grandma's garden as he refilled the feeders. As soon as he returned to the house, I counted the redbirds as they returned to their afternoon meal. Twenty-two bright red males, plus their mates, landed in the white snow around the feeders and shared the seed that Grandpa had left for them.

"They are normally territorial birds," Grandma said, looking out the window over my shoulder. "But they know that Grandpa will keep plenty of food out there for them, so they don't fight when they come to our farm." I was content to sit and watch them until it was time to go home. Thus another child was introduced to the fascinating pastime of watching birds.

By watching the birds, I learned that natural enemies are friendly to each other when there is plenty of food for them. When I later learned that Jesus Christ came to give us abundant life, I remembered how abundant seed caused the birds to be at peace. So I looked further into the life of Jesus to see what else He had to say. " 'Look at the birds of the air,' " He once said, " 'they do not sow or reap or store away in barns, and yet your heavenly Father feeds them. Are you not much more valuable than they?' " (Matthew 6:26).

I read these words when I was the last one left at home with my single-parent mother. We needed a promise of provision, and I believed this uncomplicated truth that God would care for us, and He did.

Mother always had a bird feeder some-where in our yard. There were times she must have used the "widow's mite" to pay for seed, but such a heritage as feeding birds is one that a person finds ways to finance. Whenever we had to move to a new home, she would search the trees for a cardinal to confirm her choice. Without fail, we would either hear one singing or see one sweep by in answer to her prayers. If there were redbirds nearby, she knew we could be happy there, and we always were.

Now it's my turn to feed the birds. My hus-band, James, loves to watch them as much as I do. We buy one hundred pounds of black-oil sunflower seed and twenty pounds of thistle every month from the farmer's co-op in our suburb. Every morning, I distribute four quarts of seed to four feeders and top off two finch feeders with the thistle. I recently started to ration the seed because each night the raccoons finish off whatever amount is left.

One night two adult raccoons and nine babies were foraging through our feeders. When I finally understood how much seed these masked marauders were eating, I began leaving a truce offering of leftovers at the fence for them. They love watermelon and spaghetti!

We live in the middle of a large city, but we see quail, rabbits, possums, owls, hawks, and even a blue heron that fishes at the creek in our backyard greenbelt. Hummingbirds finally started visiting our feeder just as I began working with Joy on this book. For some reason, they suddenly agreed with its location when I moved the feeder to the window by our back door. I can stand within inches of them and watch them through the window while they eat.

When the snow falls, we've counted as many as thirty-five finches eating together. This spring an indigo bunting, a goldfinch, and a purple finch fed together at the thistle feeder. Red, blue, and yellow birds festively displayed God's creativity! Over the years, various birds have caused us to stop near a window and take notice that the world is rich with life beyond our daily routine.

We have grown fond of many pets in our backyard. A mockingbird sings in the night when I am sleepless. Ravens wake me in the morning as they gather their family for their daily search for food. The Bible says that ravens call unto God for their food (see Job 38:41), and He hears their cry and feeds them (see Psalm 147:9). A wren chirps to let me know the feeders are empty, then hustles back to building his nest; the first year in our chiminea, the next in our barbecue grill, and finally in the birdhouse that says "bed and breakfast," where we enjoyed watching his babies grow this year. Our two turtledoves from last summer have multiplied to twenty that flutter to the trees when I open the back door. Sometimes I open the door just to hear their wings whistle. Of course, the redbirds are first to come to the feeder in the morning and last to visit at night, letting me know that even though life is full of constant change, some of the more pleasant events of the day remain the same.

The beauty assistant at my hairstylist's told me how her husband called from his work site one morning when she was extremely busy at the salon. Several patrons were waiting with critical solutions in their hair that would need to be rinsed when the timers went off. She told the receptionist she would have to call him back, but he insisted that she come to the phone, just for a second! Thinking it must be an emergency, she took the portable phone as she continued to watch the timers carefully.

"Listen!" her husband said excitedly from his construction site. "Can you hear that mockingbird singing? Isn't it beautiful?"

"Yeah, Honey, it's great," she said, realizing what a wonderful guy she was married to. They hadn't heard a mockingbird since they had moved to their current rental home. The sound of the bird brought back great memories of happy times and somehow reassured them that things would settle down and there would be other mockingbirds to enjoy together soon.

Later he told her, "I just felt like God wanted me to call you." I personally believe that more marriages would make it through tough challenges if couples would stop more often to consider the birds.

A few years ago, while teaching at a writers' conference, I told conferees that I would like to see personal experience stories based on their hobbies and special interests. I believed that spiritual lessons could be drawn from our encounters in God's creation and through activities that we enjoy. Setting forth the challenge, I announced, "Send your stories to me and I will add the parables I see in them that illustrate lessons from God's Word."

I was so pleased when Joy sent her collection of bird stories to me. I watch birds, but Joy *sees* them. Her perceptive observations set the stage for rich examples of God's love for us. We *are* more valuable to Him than the birds. As we watch the birds gather their daily bread, we should remember that God also cares for us.

Though I encourage you to read all the stories in this book, it does not need to be read all at once. Instead, it should be read often, to refresh and restore your hope in God. As you read our book, you will see why Jesus told us in Matthew 6 to look at the birds. He always taught with parables; when He wanted to show us how to trust God, I believe He chose birds as an example because everyone in the world has access to these feathered ideals of God's provision. Let their morning praise songs remind us that we cannot add a single hour to our life by worrying; instead, we, too, should celebrate a new day knowing that our heavenly Father knows exactly what we need and has promised to take care of us.

A Note from Joy

My mother and I often watch the humming-birds at my feeders as we visit with each other. One day, a tiny bird suddenly took a wrong turn and flew into the window. We rushed outside to see if anything could be done for it.

The female ruby-throated hummingbird lay motionless on the deck floor. Her neck was bent at a strange angle.

"Gently rub her back," Mom told me. I sat down beside the bird, fearing my touch could cause more injury. With one finger, I rubbed the bird's tiny back and prayed out loud, "Lord, please heal this creature. You made her and know that we need You right now!"

A few seconds later, the bird moved its head into a different position. Then she fluttered her wings. She was alive!

The new position allowed me to rub her chest. The bird settled in toward my touch and went to sleep! I picked her up and placed her in the palm of my hand. She rested there, blinked a couple of times, and then flew to a nearby branch. Soon she flew to the feeder for a drink.

Looking back at this event, I remember the

awe I felt for the Lord, who had answered my prayer for a tiny bird. As I held her in the palm of my hand, I was keenly aware that He holds me in His.

Sometimes life is full of more falls than flying. When down, we should learn to call out to the Lord for help. Just as God knew the tiny bird—even to the number of her iridescent feathers—He knows us, too—even the number of hairs on our heads. He knows our anxieties and sorrows, and the joys and victories He has planned for us. He is an ever-present help in trouble, who promises to answer us when we call upon Him.

A few years ago, at the Florida Christian Writers' Conference in Titusville, one of the editors (Cristine Bolley) invited us to send her any bird stories we had. I later sent her a few of my personal encounters with my feathered friends and, in time, those stories grew into this book.

Each story offers an illustration of God's ability to teach us lessons through His creation. At the end of the stories you will find three points to consider—the Bird Feeder, the Birdbath, and the Birdhouse.

The section called "Bird Feeder" offers a

seed of wisdom to meditate upon while considering the truth of the story. Both the Old and New Testaments are filled with reassurance that God will send manna to His people on a daily basis. He also promises to send wisdom for each new situation that we face.

The "Birdbath" section reflects the cleansing and refreshment that come from His Living Water, the Truth of His Word. Just as we cannot live without real water, we cannot enjoy the abundant life without knowing the truth of God's promises.

And finally, as we look at the "Birdhouse" section, we are reminded that wisdom, understanding, and knowledge are applied to our lives through the power of prayer. By living in a "house of prayer," we can apply the truth of each lesson to our own lives.

Like the bird sanctuary in my yard, I welcome you to flit in for a bite and fly out with the breath of God beneath your wings! When this book was nearly finished, we moved back to the city. Worried about the birds that fed in my yard, before we moved, I slowly weaned them from the feeders and birdbath. Settling into our new house the first day, I wondered how long it would be before I could get our new feeders up.

I was lonely for the birds I had left behind. I looked out the window while washing the dishes and there in the crab apple tree were chickadees! Drying my hands and thanking God for the delightful little birds, I walked to the deck doors. There on the big oak tree was a downy woodpecker and a nuthatch. More thanksgiving filled my heart.

Then I walked to another window and saw a wren and two purple finches. I heard the soft song of a "mourning" dove. I watched robins from yet another window as they worked the ground for breakfast. Canada geese flew overhead. Sparrows and redpolls chipped and chirped from the evergreen. I just had to keep looking!

At another window, I watched a blue jay, and in a nearby tree was a family of crows. Finally, upstairs in my office, my heart full of joy, I saw a male cardinal sit outside the window and sing his sweet spring song at the top of his voice. My cup overflowed.

Looking out our new windows that day, I felt God gently welcome me into our new home. I knew He understood the desire of my heart and wondered, *Lord, does my delight bring You joy?* I do know He reaffirmed my faith and my desire to share these experiences with you. As you hear the birds call in your neighborhood, remember that God loves you and is thinking of you. It is my prayer that these essays will bring you closer to the One who created the birds of the air and saw that it was good!

Acknowledgments

We would like to acknowledge Joy's husband, Jon, and Cristine's husband, James, for keeping their wives supplied with birdseed and for sharing our fascination with birds. We thank you for listening to our stories and contributing to the lessons hidden in these encounters.

To Joy's friends and to Cristine's daughters, Lindsey, Erin, and Jamie, we thank you for your love, patience, and encouragement while we worked on this manuscript.

Thank you, Barbour Publishing, Inc., for sharing our vision and giving us the opportunity to inspire awareness of God's lessons through His creation.

And to the Lord for blessing us with personal encounters with birds and teaching us His life's lessons through them.

A Drink of Dew

I FILL our birdbaths in the morning. The moist grass soaks my shoes while my feathered friends whistle and sing from nearby branches. When I finish, they flit about, taking turns drinking the fresh water. The goldfinches and chickadees ignore the birdbath, preferring to get their morning drinks a different way. The finches work the blades of grass for precious drops of dew. They stretch their necks as their tiny beaks move up the slender strands of green. On the nearby trees, black-capped chickadees maneuver for the best spot to reach the glistening beads of moisture on the leaves— even if it means hanging upside down to do it!

I wake up looking for refreshment, too. Each morning, my soul thirsts for a Word from God. I have learned I can bathe in His life-giving water by reading the Bible. The verses work their way into my heart and teach me of God's precepts.

Sometimes the words pierce my self-awareness and bring me to admit my wrong-doings and regrets. Most often the words remind me of God's unfailing love and provision. After drinking in His good news and soaking in the truth of His love, I can begin my day with a full cup.

Sometimes, I am not able to spend luxurious time bathing in God's Word. Then, like the finches and chickadees, I know I can still find God's refreshment, even if it means stretching and reaching a bit. I may even have to go "out on a limb" for a glistening drop of encouragement; but if I look for Him, I always find the eternal Living Water waiting for me within reach.

BIRD FEEDER:

When our thirsty soul is not quenched, we may need to turn over a new leaf to find the water that satisfies us.

BIRDBATH:

"Jesus stood and said in a loud voice, 'If anyone is thirsty, let him come to me and drink. Whoever believes in me, as the Scripture has said, streams of living water will flow from within him.' By this he meant the Spirit, whom those who believed in him were later to receive. Up to that time the Spirit had not been given, since Jesus had not yet been glorified" (John 7:37–39).

BIRDHOUSE:

Lord, because I believe in You,
my thirst is quenched by Your Holy Spirit,
who faithfully reminds me of
Your unconditional love.

FOR THE BIRDS:

Keep a shallow pie pan filled with fresh water on the ground for tiny birds such as goldfinches and chickadees. Finches love to swing from covered wire loops near their feeders while waiting their turn to eat. Chickadees will occasionally try thistle from the finch feeders especially made to hold tiny kernels of seed.

A Lesson in Love

UPSET WITH my husband, I stormed outside to cool off. On the deck a pair of cardinals landed at the feeders. The female approached first. When she was sure it was safe, she called to her mate. In a brilliant flash, he joined her and immediately reached for a sunflower seed. "Just like a man!" I fumed.

Then, to my surprise, he broke open the seed and fed it to his mate. She returned the favor. Between bites, they gently rubbed beaks, then flew off together.

All the books I've read on marriage were not as profound as the lesson the redbirds taught me that day. In their normal routine of eating, the cardinals reminded me it is important to put our mates first. Shame and longing to be forgiven for my hasty anger sent me racing back into the house. While calling my husband's name, I cried out to God in my heart, begging His forgiveness, too.

Later that summer, a pair of cardinals brought their young to the same feeder. The female stood guard over her family while the male patiently taught the demanding little birds the art of seed cracking. From time to time, the female came in for a seed, then headed back to her perch. Neither bird hesitated to serve their young or each other. For them it meant survival; for me it was a lesson in love.

BIRD FEEDER:

Because we are made in the image of God, we are happiest when loving others and looking after their needs.

BIRDBATH:

"You, my brothers, were called to be free. But do not use your freedom to indulge the sinful nature; rather, serve one another in love" (Galatians 5:13).

BIRDHOUSE:
*Lord, keep me alert to moments when
I can let others go first.*

FOR THE BIRDS:
At least forty species of birds will eat black-oil sunflower seeds that can be purchased inexpensively in large quantities. Striped sunflower seed has a tougher shell and is more suitable for larger birds. Cracked corn is a favorite addition for many birds. As an occasional treat, look for seed mixes with dried mixed fruit or a cherry flavoring on it.

Apple Blossom Time

THE SWEET scent of apple blossoms filled the air after the gentle rain. A quiet, warm breeze caught the fragrance and carried it into the house through my opened windows. Suddenly the air was filled with the familiar sound of many birds. I raced out of the house just as my husband stepped out of his shop. The birds' songs were so loud, he had heard them above the clamor of his work. He looked at me with eyebrows raised.

"Cedar waxwings," I whispered.

We headed to the other side of the garage, where the sound came from. The apple tree was full of hungry cedar waxwings. The tired and gentle birds let us get close to them while they devoured the blossoms. We let them feast, and just as well, since they are known to eat until they can eat no more.

As I turned away, a dart of deep blue near the feeders caught my attention. A tiny indigo bunting settled to eat thistle seed. I sat in my chair beside him and marveled that he had overcome his shyness to visit our feeder. This delightful songster is more often found along roadsides. They eat insects in the summer and weed seeds in the fall and winter. Spring must have caught him in between food supplies. He, too, seemed starved.

Suddenly a flash of red, brighter than a cardinal, swept towards our crab apple tree, where a scarlet tanager now rested among the pink blossoms. Another rare sighting in our yard!

A few weeks prior, I had studied these birds in my books. I knew the indigo bunting and scarlet tanagers were regulars in the woods, but I'd never seen either one. I also loved the cedar waxwings and longed to see them again. So, I prayed that day and asked God to send them into my life. He brought them all on one day! What are the odds of that?

My hunger for God causes me to ask for things that only He can satisfy. Hunger also motivated the little birds to follow God's lead to my yard, where food awaited them. God met their needs and mine in one fell swoop of love. When the birds moved on, our yard seemed strangely quiet. Their songs had filled more than the air—they had filled our hearts with reassurance of God's love.

BIRD FEEDER:
Hunger motivates us to try new things; may we never become so satisfied that we miss an adventure with God.

BIRDBATH:
"He humbled you, causing you to hunger and then feeding you with manna, which neither you nor your fathers had known, to teach you that man does not live on bread alone but on every word that comes from the mouth of the LORD" (Deuteronomy 8:3).

BIRDHOUSE:
Lord, help me follow You to places that will satisfy my hunger of wanting to know You more.

FOR THE BIRDS:

It is normal for up to twenty cedar waxwings to fly together in search for food. Plant pyracantha, cotoneaster shrubs, and mountain ash trees if you want to attract these beautiful birds to your house.

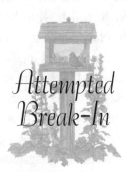

Attempted Break-In

"DID YOU see the police cars in the driveway?" our neighbor Don asked.

"No," I responded with peaked interest.

Only four houses line the gravel road to our house, and police cars are not the norm. My neighbor went on to explain the damage done to his back door. Large chunks of wood littered the deck, and it looked like someone had used a chisel to get in the house.

"Apparently the intruder fled when he heard me inside," he concluded. Someone mentioned that criminals often return to the scene of the crime when they don't get what they were after. Don was determined to protect his house from any further invasion. Unsettled, we returned to our homes and I made sure the lock was secure behind me.

Finally, the intruder did indeed return and tried diligently to finish what he had started.

It was only a few days later when my neighbor heard a loud pounding again at the screen door. Surprised by the boldness of the thief returning in daylight, yet determined to stop the robber once and for all, Don crept quietly to the door. Suddenly eye-to-eye with his destructive intruder, my neighbor sighed with relief and grinned at the pileated woodpecker perched on the deck door handle.

The otherwise quiet bird was shredding what was left of the cedar trim around Don's door. His grasp was awkward, but he was determined to get every last bug that might be hiding in the doorway.

Evidence often leads us to the wrong conclusions. We were fooled by the woodpecker's clues. He wasn't trying to get in; instead, he was trying to get some tiny bugs out of Don's door for lunch. We assumed the wood chips and damaged door would lead to a burglar. Our faith was misplaced.

We make these same mistakes with our assumptions about God. We assume we know all there is to know about Him. Many who approach God see Him only as the righteous judge and turn away from Him in fear they can never measure up to His standard. A closer look at the evidence shows us that His standard, Jesus, lowered Himself to be like us so that we could come to Him.

Some see the death of God's Son, Jesus, on a cross only as an act of brutality, when in fact it was an extreme sacrifice of unconditional love from the only One capable of giving us life. Yet, if people assume the life of Jesus ended on a piece of splintered wood, they will not know to answer the knock at the door when our risen Savior comes to live with them.

Bird Feeder:
Believing a lie gives it the power to fill us with fear.

Birdbath:
"To the Jews who had believed him, Jesus said, 'If you hold to my teaching, you are really my disciples. Then you will know the truth, and the truth will set you free'" (John 8:31–32).

BIRDHOUSE:
When fear enters my heart,
I will ask You, Lord,
for truth and be set free.

FOR THE BIRDS:
Hairy or red-headed woodpeckers will make their home in a house with a base that is 6" x 6" wide. The entrance hole needs to be 2" wide and 10" up from the bottom of the nest to give them plenty of room to raise their babies.

Aunt Goose

ONE SPRING day, while walking around the lake, I saw a family of Canada geese. The downy babies had no fear of me, so I was able to get close to them. I watched their sleeping parents and wondered why they didn't chase me away.

Suddenly from behind me came a threatening hiss! The goslings headed for the protective wings of their parents, and I turned slowly around. A big, white farm goose stretched her neck and repeated her warning. I moved away.

From a safe distance, I watched the goose family and their imposing white guard. The birds had an understanding. The goose with no family of her own took charge of this one. Like a sentry at Buckingham Palace, she paced the area, head raised, eyes always watching.

A couple of weeks later, I returned to the lake. The white goose still kept her eyes on the now gawky goslings. When they wandered out of their invisible safety zone, she would let out a warning "Honk!" The young geese quickly returned to their parents.

Like the white goose, for reasons beyond our control, we are sometimes without our own family. Or like the goslings, we wander beyond the borders of safety in this life. Aunt Goose's honks and hisses warned the parents and brought the little ones back into line. Likewise, God sends the Holy Spirit to guide us away from danger and warn us about temptation.

David, the young shepherd who was appointed by God to become king of the Jews, knew a great deal about danger. His predecessor, Saul, wanted him dead, but God spared David's life because he trusted the Lord. Psalm 91:11–16 is David's journal of discovery that God had commanded His angels to guard those who love Him.

God spoke to David about those who believe on His name, saying, "Because he has set his love upon Me, therefore will I deliver him; I will set him on high, because he knows *and* understands My name [has a personal knowledge of My mercy, love, and kindness—trusts and relies on Me, knowing I will never forsake him, no never]. He shall call upon Me, and I will answer him; I will be with him in trouble, I will deliver him and honor him. With long life will I satisfy him and show him My salvation" (Psalm 91:14–16 AMPLIFIED).

BIRD FEEDER:
We all need a hiss or a honk now and then to bring us back into the safety of our Father's love.

BIRDBATH:
[Jesus said,] " 'And I will ask the Father, and he will give you another Counselor [the Holy Spirit] to be with you forever' " (John 14:16).

BIRDHOUSE:
Thank You for angels to protect me, and Your Spirit who leads me away from danger.

FOR THE BIRDS:

Old bread, including donuts, is never wasted if thrown to the geese. Sparrows, blackbirds, pheasants, quail, and ducks all enjoy these treats, too! Keep leftovers in the freezer, and when the bag is full, head for a nearby lake or pond where geese are known to be.

Birth Announcement

ONE SPRING morning a wren fluttered around me at the bird feeders.

"What do you want, little fellow?" I asked the persistent visitor. He flew back and forth, singing. I followed him to the wren house nestled into the grapevines growing up the arbor. He waited for me on top of the house. Nothing in his actions showed fear or a need for help. He cocked his head and listened. The female joined him.

From inside came the sounds of tiny baby wrens. I was hearing their first songs! Soon, Mama returned to the little ones and Papa went in search of food.

Leaving their house in the vines, I smiled. The wrens seemed to be celebrating the birth of their babies. Could it be? Later that day they chased me away from their little house. Walking away, I felt little doubt about their earlier intentions—they had wanted to tell someone their good news.

Good news is worth singing about. God was so excited about the birth of Jesus that He sent out announcements centuries before His arrival. Angels flew about, calling attention to many people when Jesus was born. The first angel came to a young virgin girl named Mary to announce His arrival into her womb, and later to her fiancé to reassure him that his bride-to-be had done nothing wrong. Mary had been chosen to deliver the Christ Child into the world. Nine months later, the angels heralded the news to the shepherds. Then a bright star led the wise men to His home so they, too, could look upon the new song that had been sent into the world.

His birth began centuries of "rebirth announcements" as people found new life from putting their trust in Him. God calls our attention to those who put their hope in Christ; to the first twelve disciples who later proclaimed His message to thousands; to the broken woman beside a well who found forgiveness for her way of life; and even to a thief who hung on a cross next to Jesus but later met Him in paradise!

BIRD FEEDER:
"Happy Re-birthday" is one of God's favorite songs.

BIRDBATH:
" 'In the same way, I tell you, there is rejoicing in the presence of the angels of God over one sinner who repents' " (Luke 15:10).

BIRDHOUSE:
Great was the day that I put my trust in You, Lord.

FOR THE BIRDS:
A birdhouse box that has a 4" x 4" base with an entrance that is 7" up from the bottom of the nest will serve many species of birds. Chickadees and wrens will use a house with a 1⅛"

entrance. Nuthatches and downy woodpeckers need an opening that is $1\frac{3}{8}$". The tufted titmouse will nest in a box that has a $1\frac{1}{4}$" entrance. Line the nests with wood chips if you are trying to attract chickadees, nuthatches, or downy woodpeckers.

Call of
the Wild

ONE OF my favorite outings is going to the park and feeding the giant Canada geese. I am exhilarated by their presence on all sides of me, even after forty years of visits to them. Their beauty amazes me, and for a moment I sense the pleasure of becoming their "provider" worthy of their affection. They love dried corn or day-old bread, although stale popcorn is always accepted. Hundreds of geese crowd my legs and demand attention. Mallards and pigeons scurry among the bigger birds, hoping for their share.

They honk, squabble, and bite each other in their push to get the most. Feathers and dust sometimes fly. I throw handfuls to the crowd, then offer the brave ones in front a treat from my hand. After a while, I leave a pile for the ones too eager for my attention, and I move deeper into the crowd to reach the more timid birds.

Their graceful necks, spectacular markings, and downy feathers are within my reach. But if I should reach beyond their boundaries, I'm sure to get a hiss. A bite or wing spanking is not uncommon if they feel threatened. These are wild birds, and we have a short peace agreement. I bring the treats; they allow me to be in their midst. When the food is gone, so are they. I am left alone with only a messy reminder of their presence, still on the bottom of my shoes.

Bird Feeder:
What part of us remains with God after He satisfies our hunger?

Birdbath:
"Then Jacob made a vow, saying, 'If God will be with me and will watch over me on this journey I am taking and will give me food to eat and clothes to wear so that I return safely

to my father's house, then the LORD will be my God and this stone that I have set up as a pillar will be God's house, and of all that you give me I will give you a tenth'" (Genesis 28:20–22).

BIRDHOUSE:
*I have not been hungry since
I put my faith in You.*

FOR THE BIRDS:
It's fun to give the birds and critters a special treat at Thanksgiving and Christmas. Dried fruits, nuts of all kinds, popcorn, crackers (the squirrels like Goldfish!), bits of cookies, apple chunks, pretzels, any flavor bread (banana nut is a favorite!), dog food, cracked corn, and sunflower seeds all attract guests to the holiday smorgasbord. For whatever reason, they usually share this treat together peaceably.

Cat's Meow!

I HEARD a yowling cat near the bird feeders—usually cats stalk the feeders silently. I saw only birds. The meowing continued, so I entered the woods to search for what I was convinced must be a suffering animal. If I did find it, I hoped I could help it. The woods became silent. I stood still for a few moments and the chatter began again except for the cat sounds.

A few days later I saw a slender, gray bird with a black cap on our deck. He opened his mouth and meowed! *Excuse me?* Then as he gained confidence, the yowling started. This was the "cat" I had searched for. Instead of a hurting animal, I had been on the trail of an imitator. I called my husband to tell him about the "Great Pretender" sitting on the railing.

Sometimes I, too, pretend. I deny hurt until it becomes anger. Or worse, I pretend to trust God but secretly let anxiety govern my response to trials in my life. We can imitate faith by saying all the right words, but real faith *acts* on what is spoken. I can sound like a follower of God, but the proof is my willingness to follow Him in loving acts toward people whom He loves, even unlovable ones. It's easier to pretend these aren't my responsibility.

The catbird convinced me he was something he was not. Pretending to be a Christian by talking the talk without walking the walk leads to weariness and frustration. Life's sweetness is dimmed. But when I fully lean on, rely on, and put my entire being in Him, I am restored to authenticity and my true song is again heard in our woods.

BIRD FEEDER:
It's easy to roar like a lion until a real one stands beside you.

BIRDBATH:

"Know *and* understand that it is [really] the people [who live] by faith who are [the true] sons of Abraham. And if you belong to Christ [are in Him Who is Abraham's Seed], then you are Abraham's offspring and [spiritual] heirs according to the promise" (Galatians 3:7, 29 AMPLIFIED).

BIRDHOUSE:

May people know that I am Your disciple, Lord, by the love that rules in my life.

FOR THE BIRDS:

Supplemental feeding helps birds survive, since many species lose 80 percent of their young the first year of life. Crushed eggshells help egg-laying females in the spring. Bake shells for twenty minutes at 250° to kill salmonella bacteria. Let cool and crush the shells until the pieces are smaller than a dime.

Caw

THE CROWS in our woods greet the sunrise with raucous calls. These big black birds are family oriented. Last year's brood helps raise the next batch of young before leaving to start their own families. They often nest in the same territory as their parents.

This spring I watched a crow family raise a strong-willed youngster. He refused to feed himself when his siblings did. Sitting on a branch near his family, he constantly squawked, "Caw—caw." The others moved away while his parents called him to eat. Finally one of the birds would bring him a bite, but he was never satisfied. This went on for days. I called him Caw and prayed he would eat—it was the only way I was going to get any peace and quiet!

After a week of being intermittently coaxed and ignored, he joined his family on the ground, still demanding to be fed. There was nothing any of us could do—this was one stiff-necked crow!

I watched Caw remain on the sidelines crying and begging for someone to take care of him. He annoyed me! I thought, *He is just like some people I know!* Conviction filled my soul— why is it so easy to see someone else's toothpick when a tree trunk is still in my own eye? How often have I catered to self-pity, cawing from the sidelines, "Why doesn't anyone care about me–me–meee?"

Caw was always welcome to the feast, but he had wasted his time and energy grumbling. When his family was filled and ready to explore the fields for trinkets and treasures to store in their nests, he was still hungry and frustrated. Eventually Caw stopped his noisy grumbling, pecked at a kernel of corn, and swallowed. The crows welcomed him with softer sounds and settled in around him for breakfast.

"Sorry, Lord," I whispered in prayer. "Teach me to be like Caw's siblings, looking after the younger ones in the faith instead of looking for spiritual handouts." I asked Him to forgive me for selfish thoughts and remind me of Caw the next time I feel like complaining from the sidelines!

Bird Feeder:
The mentor continues to grow as she feeds her protégé.

Birdbath:
"Each of you should look not only to your own interests, but also to the interests of others" (Philippians 2:4).

Birdhouse:
Cleanse me, Lord, from selfish ambition and give me eyes that see the needs of others.

For the Birds:
Fruit-bearing trees and shrubs help to feed and protect birds. Strawberries, gooseberries, serviceberries, and blueberries are fun to grow for their use. Dogwoods, magnolia, viburnums, roses, and honeysuckle provide edible seed for birds while adding beauty to our yards.

Cedar Waxwings

EARLY MORNING walks on the trails near our home are usually peaceful. One morning the brambles and trees along the blacktop path were full of noise. On the branches were hundreds of tired cedar waxwings. I stopped, and several incoming birds landed by my shoulder at eye level. I could have touched the weary travelers. Their bodies and song surrounded me—I felt like I was in the woodland wonderland from the scene in Disney's *Sleeping Beauty*.

They feasted on the drying berries of the bushes, and my presence was still welcome. I whispered to them, "Hello."

The bird nearest me cocked his head and moved closer to me. Somehow he knew it was

safe. Within minutes, a jogger came up behind us and the birds took flight. I could feel
the air move from the sudden flutter of their
wings. I stood still and waited, somehow sens-
ing that they might return. Then, just as I had
hoped, they settled in around me again.

Some cheeped, some ate, and some went
to sleep. I was so close that I could see individ-
ual feathers on their taupe bodies. Soon their
sounds stopped while, except for a few watch
birds, the flock rested. I stood in their midst,
enjoying the same peace they had found.

When it was time for me to head for home,
I spoke again, "Good-bye, beautiful birds."
Walking away, I whispered a prayer of thanksgiving for the peace that sometimes comes to
us on the wings of a bird.

BIRD FEEDER:
Good things come to those who learn to wait.

BIRDBATH:
"Satisfy us in the morning with your unfailing

love, that we may sing for joy and be glad all our days" (Psalm 90:14).

BIRDHOUSE:
When I am still, Lord,
Your peace settles in around me.

FOR THE BIRDS:
Migrating birds need high fat (lipid) content to provide energy for their spring flight. Magnolia trees, spicebush, flowering dogwood, and sassafras offer high-lipid fruits. Plants that offer food for fall migration include the wild rambling rose, viburnum, hawthorn, the blue-black berry of junipers, and the red berries of a yaupon holly.

Cha-peep!

MOVING OUT of the city was a lonely time for me. I was used to busy streets and human voices. Longing for company in the woods, I bought bird feeders and many varieties of seeds. I hung several finch feeders filled to the brim with thistle. A few days later, the yard was full of song and bright yellow birds.

One of the males caught my eye. He was bigger than the rest and willing to wait his turn to eat. The others were usually settling in for the night when he was finally feeding.

Early one morning he sat on the feeder pole and sang out, "Cha-peep!" I sang his song back to him. He moved closer and seemed to enjoy my company.

The next morning I wondered if he would answer my call. "Cha-peep," I called to my new friend.

Instantly I heard him echo, "Cha-peep." Each day I would call and he would come.

As spring became summer, a tiny female joined him at the feeders. Soon, two baby goldfinches came with them, and I watched as they taught their young to eat the tiny seeds. As my pool of finch friends grew, so did my love for our secluded country home. The days flew and it was suddenly time for Cha-peep and his family to migrate to a warmer climate for the winter. He was gone, but so was my loneliness; he had proven there are new friends to meet wherever we wind up in life.

BIRD FEEDER:
God never migrates or leaves us alone.

BIRDBATH:
"He that dwelleth in the secret place of the most High shall abide under the shadow of the Almighty" (Psalm 91:1 KJV).

BIRDHOUSE:
*When I call unto You, Lord,
You are quick to answer.*

FOR THE BIRDS:
Feeders need occasional cleaning. A sponge on a wire is great for cleaning the liquid feeders. Others can be sprayed with a garden hose and left to dry overnight. Be sure to refill them early the next morning. Jelly cups, often mounted on a pole, need a drop of dish soap and a small brush to scrub them. Always rinse thoroughly.

Chick & Dee

TWO CHICKADEES waited on one empty feeder while I filled the other. Their trust surprised me. Many of these little black-capped birds eat at our feeders, but none were as tame as these two. I called the little one Chick. A tiny tuft of feathers stuck out of the top of his head like a wayward cowlick. The bigger bird, named Dee, watched over the other one.

My filling of the birdbath didn't frighten them away. Chick and Dee always came together and seemed to enjoy each other's company. I often see arguments break out between the birds at our busy feeders as they fight over whose turn it is or who reached for the best seed first. Yet with all the activity, these two friends never squabbled over territory or food.

Sometimes the news seems full of stories of people fighting for certain rights. It is easy to let righteous anger become a constant defense and walk through life with our "dukes up." But in time, those who fight can become overwhelmed by their battles. As road rage grows more common, so do stomach ulcers, headaches, and sore jaws. It is also easy to forget that our rights come with responsibility.

I admire the simple life of Chick and Dee. They fly in, eat, and then leave together. They face all the same dangers and concerns other chickadees face—yet they are at peace.

I thought about my friends who have agreed together in prayer for special needs. Trials soon became testimonies. Chaos became calm. Pride and anger evaporated. Friendship overcomes fighting and peace reigns supreme when hearts are united in faith. Chick and Dee are evidence that friendship makes a difference.

BIRD FEEDER:
"If one falls down, his friend can help him up" (Ecclesiastes 4:10).

BIRDBATH:

" 'Again, I tell you that if two of you on earth agree about anything you ask for, it will be done for you by my Father in heaven. For where two or three come together in my name, there am I with them' " (Matthew 18:19–20).

BIRDHOUSE:

Lord, You are the friend that is closer than a brother.

FOR THE BIRDS:

Some birdbaths are too deep for certain birds that can drown in small amounts of water. If possible, have two birdbaths: one for the bigger birds and another with a flat rock in the center for smaller birds. They will know the difference.

Church
in the Badlands

My family stopped at a small motel nestled in the South Dakota Badlands. After a night of baseball-sized hail and rolling thunder, silence woke me at four o'clock Sunday morning. I got ready for the day while my family continued to sleep.

Outside I sat on an old log and waited. Clutching my Bible in my hands, I knew there would soon be enough sunshine to read. A soft yellow band of light broke over the rugged hills. A moment later, the sky was streaked with a wash of tangerine and lavender. The rhythmic sounds of the bugs were replaced when one lone meadowlark flew to a nearby fence post and opened his throat to the heavens. Immediately others joined him and a few soft calls from the killdeer blended in.

Not able to withhold my feeling of adoration, I, too, stood and joined in whispering a few choruses of praise to the Lord. Now the bright orb of the sun reached over the mountains and I sat down. Surrounded by the singing birds, I read God's Word. After a time of prayerful mention of all that I was thankful for, I returned to the room and my family.

The Lord provided me with a church in the wilderness of the Badlands. The still small voice of the Lord had been my call to worship when the quiet of the morning disturbed my sleep. His Word was my sermon, the birds my choir—with a meadowlark as their worship leader. The rugged rocks formed my sanctuary, and an old log became my pew.

Bird Feeder:
God has always preferred a mobile temple.

BIRDBATH:
"My voice shalt thou hear in the morning, O LORD; in the morning will I direct my prayer unto thee, and will look up" (Psalm 5:3 KJV).

BIRDHOUSE:
Thank You for choosing to live within the hearts of Your people.

FOR THE BIRDS:
Old boxes of cereal emptied on the ground will be cleaned up before your own breakfast is over. Leftover popcorn disappears quickly when left at the bird feeders. Even that last serving of peas and corn that no one eats at dinner will not be wasted if thrown out to the birds.

City Park

SITTING IN my parents' backyard doesn't feel like I'm in a suburb of a major city. It is more like relaxing in a small town park. A bench, picnic table, and swing offer choices for seeing the yard from different angles. Bird feeders line their yard, hang in trees, and dangle from their clothesline pole.

Each year, hundreds of goldfinches choose this spot as their favorite dining place. The trees are so full of the finches, they look as if they are laden with exotic yellow and black blossoms. In this homemade bird sanctuary, robins build nests, orioles teach their babies to eat grape jelly, chickadees flit about the trees, cardinals raise their families, yellow-headed blackbirds trill from the lilac bushes while blue jays warn the others if a cat or hawk invades their territory.

Mom and Dad's dog, Tasha, guards the yard by listening for the alarm of the blue jay, making sure neighborhood cats stay on the other side of her fence. When the birds hear the blue jay's warning song, they move to higher ground and watch. Tasha rushes into the yard like a bomber on a mission. With the enemy banished, Tasha makes her way back to the house and the blue jay sounds the all clear. The other birds flock back to the feeders. The yard fills with song. The safe refuge is once again theirs.

Those who have a personal knowledge of God's mercy, love, and kindness enjoy the same peace that the birds enjoy in my parents' yard. God promises to watch over those who trust and rely on Him. Like the blue jay, His Spirit calls out to us, both alerting us to impending danger and calling us to safer branches in high places.

BIRD FEEDER:

It is good to enter the sanctuary with thanksgiving.

BIRDBATH:

"If you make the Most High your dwelling—
even the LORD, who is my refuge—then no
harm will befall you, no disaster will come near
your tent" (Psalm 91:9–10).

BIRDHOUSE:

*Give me keen ears to hear Your alarm
and quick reflexes to move to
the shelter of Your sanctuary.*

FOR THE BIRDS:

Clean the birdbath frequently with a hard
force of water from the garden hose. If moss
or fungus begins to grow in it, use dish soap
and swirl it around with a cleaning brush.
About once a month, clean the birdbath with
a small amount of bleach in warm water. Let
it sit for a few minutes, then rinse it thoroughly before refilling. An old mailbox in the
garden is a great place to store cleaning tools
and gloves.

Cleaning House

WE PUT up a martin house in the yard and watched. Scout birds would be in the area soon, and we wanted them to feel welcome. One morning, song came out of the house and a dark bird flew in and out with nesting materials. We hurried out to greet the new neighbors.

Grackles had moved in on one side and sparrows on the other. We could have been disappointed because we had heard they were noisy and messy birds. But we watched with fascination as they busily prepared apartments for their young. On a nearby wire sat a scout martin. He was too late.

For years the grackles and sparrows returned to our martin house to raise their babies. The house has a porch, and the two families sit on opposite sides undisturbed by the presence of the other.

In the spring the male and female grackle work together raising their family. Mrs. G. sits inside and Mr. G. goes hunting for food. When he brings home a tasty tidbit, his mate trades unwanted litter from inside the nest for him to carry away. Mama feeds the babies and cleans the nest. Papa hunts and takes care of the natural debris. Theirs is a partnership of responsibility.

Early in the morning, the songs of tiny grackles break the stillness—the babies are hungry. The routine begins again. Papa leaves the house and mama waits at the doorway. The privilege of being parents to their little brood brings huge responsibilities, but the grackles and sparrows don't shirk their duty.

Our favorite time to watch the house is in the evening when Mr. G. and Mr. S. (sparrow) sit on their porches. Their babies are asleep, their mates have finally stopped sending them on errands, and the two males enjoy a quiet moment outside. In spite of their busy lives, they take time to sit quietly together, perhaps reflecting on the enormity of their responsibilities and blessings—or maybe they are just thankful that their families are finally asleep.

When I see them together, I think of how Jesus said that we are to love our neighbors as ourselves. A lawyer once asked Jesus the question, "Who is my neighbor?" Jesus responded with the story of the Good Samaritan who took care of a wounded stranger (see Luke 10). The lawyer understood that a good neighbor is one who shows mercy to another person, whether a stranger or someone who lives beside them.

I look at my husband, Jon, who sits beside me on the patio, and notice that he enjoys the birds as much as I do. Thankful for our friendship, I decide not to mention the projects I had in mind for him when he asks me what I'm thinking about—at least, not tonight.

Bird Feeder:
The early bird gets the worm; the wise one gets the house and the good neighbor.

BIRDBATH:

"If it is possible, as far as it depends on you, live at peace with everyone" (Romans 12:18).

BIRDHOUSE:

*Help me to be a good neighbor
and sit quietly beside them when
they just need a friend.*

FOR THE BIRDS:

Empty birdhouses when the babies have left to make it ready for the next family. Unscrew one side of the house and clean out old nesting materials. If you don't want sparrows taking over your bluebird or martin houses, plug the entries until the preferred birds will be in the area again. Check your bird book for approximate arrival dates in your area.

Cleaning with a Cock-a-tiel

FOR A while I earned money cleaning other people's houses. One of my clients had a pet cock-a-tiel. He had a dusky gray body, yellow comb, and orange cheeks. At first I kept him in his cage, not wanting him to mess where I had cleaned.

Eventually, he and I became friends and I learned that he loved being out of the cage. I still didn't want surprise messes for the family to find, so I found a compromise, and to my amazement it worked. I put on a baseball cap and he perched on my head. (I didn't want any surprises in my hair, either!) I dusted, mopped, and scrubbed bathrooms with a bird on my hat. Cleaning demands the use of both hands, and with all my bending and walking around, it was up to him to keep his balance.

The only time he wanted nothing to do with me was when it was time to vacuum—then he gladly returned to his cage. He learned my routine; and as soon as I put my cleaning supplies away, before I even reached for the vacuum cleaner, he hopped down onto my shoulder. I offered him my finger as a perch and returned him to the cage.

Compromise kept us together, and we enjoyed each other's company. There were still limits to how far we were willing to participate in the other's lifestyle and habits, but being together when we could made us both whistle while we worked.

BIRD FEEDER:
Better is a bird on the head than two in a cage.

BIRDBATH:
"Make every effort to live in peace with all men and to be holy; without holiness no one will see the Lord. See to it that no one misses the grace of God and that no bitter root grows up to

cause trouble and defile many" (Hebrews 12:14–15).

BIRDHOUSE:

*Lord, show me ways to include others
in my life so they can witness
Your grace from my viewpoint.*

FOR THE BIRDS:

Caution: If you need to use ant killer pellets, place a small basket over a confined area with a rock on top of the basket. This will protect bug-eating birds from ingesting the poison.

Colorado Hummers

THE FIRST step onto the world's highest suspension bridge at the Royal Gorge in Colorado is hard to take. The drop to the river is 1,053 feet with rugged rocks on each side of it. The river below looks like a tiny blue piece of thread lying on the canyon floor. The dread increases when the bridge starts to sway from the movement of other people crossing it. When I reached the far side, I was eager to sit down on solid ground again where benches lined the veranda.

Once seated, I quickly forgot about my fear of high places when I saw dozens of hummingbirds sipping nectar at the feeders. Since they are usually territorial, I was amazed to see so many hummers feeding together. Some sat together while others hovered and sipped. The abundance of tourists did not frighten or distract them. When a person got in their way, they let out a short peep and swerved to miss them. Their masterful aeronautics saved them from many head-on collisions with humans seeking souvenirs and ice cream cones.

I sat still, watching them, when one small bird buzzed by close enough to cause my hair to move from the currents of its flight. Another hovered near my shoulder, inspecting me closely. One brave hummer paused for a moment near my face, and we observed each other eye-to-eye. Several fed at the feeder by my head.

The fearless hummingbirds at the Royal Gorge offer a glimpse of the relationship God wants each of us to enjoy with Him. Amos 4:13 says, "He who forms the mountains, creates the wind, and reveals his thoughts to man, he who turns dawn to darkness, and treads the high places of the earth—the LORD God Almighty is his name." God's thoughts are higher than our thoughts. He wants us to forget about "territorial rights" and fearlessly come to Him.

To enjoy God's provision in this high place, the hummers had to leave the solid ground below and fly up the canyon to the feeders.

And if we want to find God's provision, we must leave what feels like solid ground to cross over the dreaded gulf that separates us from Him.

Colossians 1:20 (TLB) explains that Jesus cleared a path for everything to come to God—all things in heaven and on earth, "for Christ's death on the cross has made peace with God for all by his blood." Christ laid down His life and became the bridge that crossed the great divide between God and mankind.

Once in God's presence, we enjoy His peace. When others witness the magnitude of God's peace in our lives, in spite of the dangers around us, they, too, will dare to walk across the suspension bridge that has been laid down for them. Soon those who were weary and afraid will be "humming" with praise just like the rest of us.

BIRD FEEDER:

When focused on the sweet presence of Jesus, Peter was able to walk on the buffeting waves that only seconds before had terrified him. (See Matthew 14:22–34.)

BIRDBATH:

"Is any one of you in trouble? He should pray. Is anyone happy? Let him sing songs of praise" (James 5:13).

BIRDHOUSE:

Thank You for revealing
Your thoughts to me, Lord,
and for keeping my feet on the solid rock.

FOR THE BIRDS:

Hummingbird and oriole feeders need fresh sugar water every few days. Mix one cup of sugar to four cups of water and bring the mixture just to the point of boiling to keep the sugar solution from spoiling. Turn the heat off as soon as it starts to boil so nutrients aren't destroyed.

Dangerous Crossing

WHEN RETURNING home from a day of shopping, my friend and I spotted twelve tiny pheasants milling around in the middle of the road. I pulled the car over and we walked toward the babies, hoping to hustle them off the road. I was certain their mother was nearby, and then we heard her call from the field. A couple of the little ones suddenly plopped down, choosing to enjoy the warmth of the blacktop and ignore her!

I knew the road was usually busy and the young birds didn't stand a chance if someone came over the hill at the speed limit. We tried again to herd them toward the ditch while their mother persistently called out to them. One little pheasant was obviously frightened and confused by our presence. He turned from the direction of his mother's call and headed the wrong way. One step and I was able to encourage him back into the flock. Just as we reached the ditch near the field where the mother waited, a car zoomed by. The babies scurried into the tall grass, never aware of the danger they avoided.

The little birds thought they were in a good place and were reluctant to respond to their mother's warning. The pavement was warm and their vision was clear because there was no tall grass to block their view. It was a great example of how dangerous it is to trust our feelings instead of simply obeying the voice of the One who loves us.

When God calls us away from comfort, we should trust His motives more than our own judgment. We can't see over the hill, but He is quick to rescue us in spite of our uncertainty. I thought about the little one whose doubt made him ready to turn back toward danger and remembered the many times God's grace kept me from doing the wrong thing.

BIRD FEEDER:
"But for grace, there go I."

BIRDBATH:
"But because of his great love for us, God, who is rich in mercy, made us alive with Christ even when we were dead in transgressions—it is by grace you have been saved" (Ephesians 2:4–5).

BIRDHOUSE:
Thank You for helping me cross to the other side.

FOR THE BIRDS:
If you have room in your yard, birds enjoy a small brush pile. Some species will nest there, giving you the opportunity to watch some usually shy birds. In the winter, small birds like juncos appreciate the shelter. A large pile may draw unwanted critters, so a small pile is recommended.

Dirt Bath

A WREN landed on the railroad tie at the edge of my wildflower garden while I was weeding the bed. I had dropped a small pile of dirt that was clumped to the roots of the weeds, and the warm sun had dried the soil to a powdery dust. It was just right for a little bird to enjoy a dirt bath. The wren watched me for a moment, decided I was no threat, and in he dove! Reveling in the warm powdered soil, he lost himself in the moment and fell off the tie onto the grass!

I couldn't help but laugh. Obviously upset, he flew to the branch above my head and scolded me! It was my fault. I left the dirt there in the first place. Forget that he had thrown caution to the wind. He finally gave up his verbal tirade and headed home.

"Silly bird!" I called after him.

Never mind that I, sometimes, behave just like the wren. When I do something foolish and wind up with dirt on my face, I would rather blame someone else, too. If I get too busy and then face deadline crunches, I want it to be someone else's fault. But if others dare to smile at my predicament, I angrily chirp at them! Then I hear a still small voice say, "Silly child! You knew to do right and chose not to—this is your problem, not theirs!"

Like the wren, I sulk for a moment because blunders are not fun, but they can be funny. The little brown wren taught me that lesson. A few minutes after his fall from the dirt bath, he was singing again. Forgotten was his humiliation and frustration and full was his song of joy again. The next time my pride looks for someone to blame, I hope I can take myself less seriously and quickly sing like a bird again!

BIRD FEEDER:
Humor is best applied when looking at past mistakes.

BIRDBATH:
"Before his downfall a man's heart is proud, but humility comes before honor" (Proverbs 18:12).

BIRDHOUSE:
Thank You for loving me, Lord, imperfections and all.

FOR THE BIRDS:
Many birds like a dust bath to rid their bodies of parasites. A dust bath can be made for them by outlining a 3' x 3' area with attractive bricks or rocks. Fill the area with an equal mix of sand, loam, and sifted ash to give them a waterless bathing pool.

Doing It Her Way

A TINY wren industriously built a nest in the new house hanging from the apple tree in the front yard. He worked from dusk to dawn choosing the right materials and checking them over carefully before entering the house with them. When he was done the next day, he sat on top of the house, tipped his little head back, and filled the air with song.

Later, he brought home his mate to inspect their nest. I was shocked when she tore the whole thing apart and started over. Twigs and grass flew out of the house and landed on the ground or floated away on the breeze. She chattered at him and he brought new supplies. She discarded most of them. If he tried to take a shortcut and bring her something she had dumped out, she threw it out again. She fluttered and sputtered at him all day.

Finally, she had what she wanted and built the nest her way. She moved in and he sat silently on the rooftop.

What a stiff-necked bird, I thought while feeling sorry for the stoic little male. It was her way or no way. Her stubborn, ungrateful heart caused her to miss the point of his thoughtfulness and careful search for a good home. *Hmmm, she was acting just like me when Jon first built me this home in the country.* Her behavior wasn't a pretty sight.

But it was the action of the male wren that spoke to my heart. He guarded her with intense passion night and day, seemingly undisturbed by her picky little ways. As I watched the wren go happily about his work, I thought, *He is just like my husband.* I realized the female wren and I both had a good thing going.

BIRD FEEDER:

Happy is the one who understands there is more than one right way to do something.

BIRDBATH:

"Love does not demand its own way. It is not irritable or touchy. It does not hold grudges and will hardly even notice when others do it wrong" (1 Corinthians 13:5 TLB).

BIRDHOUSE:

The next time I feel like moving furniture, remind me to show gratitude to those who help me.

FOR THE BIRDS:

Leave a small pile of nesting materials somewhere for your birds. Cut cotton string, colorful yarn, or baling twine into strips. Small bits of shiny metallic thread often catch the eye of a creative nester. Dog hair and human hair from a brush will add a soft lining to a nest. Add a handful of grass cuttings and small twigs to their building supplies. The pleasure of watching the birds inspect the pieces is well worth the little time it takes to gather supplies for them. Add to the pile when it dwindles, and clean it up when it seems they are finished.

Feeding the Geese

THE BOY stood in the park surrounded by Canada geese. Clutched in his hand was a small bag of cheese curls. He smiled as he looked from the bag to the birds. I couldn't hear what he was saying, but I could see that he was talking to them as he fed the big geese his crispy orange treats one at a time.

The geese were noisy and pushy, clamoring for the boy's attention. At first glimpse it appeared the geese were in control, but closer inspection revealed the boy was definitely in charge of the cheese curl distribution. Looking at the geese through thick lenses, he was careful to see that each goose received a treat—as though he knew something about the pain of being overlooked and left out.

He had walked into the park on legs enclosed in metal braces. Instead of holding onto his treat, he gave every last cheese curl away joyfully! When the bag was empty, the geese turned and waddled away. The boy smiled and made his way to the swings over the uneven ground.

With one little bag of treats he had fed a gaggle of geese.

Life sometimes surrounds us with pressures and hurts. It would be easy to hang on to the few good things we have, hoping to satisfy our own discomfort, but this little stranger reminds us of the joy that comes from sharing what we have with others whose hunger seems greater than our own.

BIRD FEEDER:

Life's greatest challenge is not in overcoming our limitations but in generously sharing our strengths.

BIRDBATH:

"Little children, let us not love [merely] in theory or in speech but in deed and in truth [in practice and in sincerity]" (1 John 3:18 AMPLIFIED).

BIRDHOUSE:

What I have I will give to You, Lord.

FOR THE BIRDS:

Wood duck houses often hold several "families" each year. When the wood ducks move out, woodpeckers and squirrels have been known to move right in.

flicker

EVERY MORNING, soon after the alarm went off, we heard pounding on the roof for several days in a row. By the time we got outside to see who was up there, they were gone. We hoped one of the pileated woodpeckers wasn't beating on the roof because he might be strong enough to cause the roof to leak.

Finally, early one morning, I was outside when the banging started again. I looked up and saw a northern flicker fervently at work on our antenna. Jon, who was inside at the time, came out to get a look at the culprit on the roof and confirmed it was the same sound we had been hearing before. Outside it had a metallic sound, inside it didn't.

Chasing the flicker away didn't work. In the end, the insistent visitor won his right to our rooftop and we were helpless against his intrusion. He just came back—usually just after Jon's car left the driveway. Eventually the flicker found what it was looking for and moved on; but until it did, we simply had to put up with the noise it created. We even had to put up a new antenna because the TV reception began fading in and out. We replaced it only when we were confident that the flicker wouldn't be back.

It seems strange, but Jesus told us to be just like that flicker when we need answers from God. When He told His followers to *ask* God for what they wanted or needed, He used the Greek word *aiteo* (pronounced *ahee-teh'-o*), which means to "ask, beg, call for, crave, desire, require." This kind of asking is much like the persistence of the flicker on our rooftop, who didn't stop pecking away at our antenna until his curiosity was completely satisfied.

The Word of God says in James 4:2, "You want something but don't get it. You kill and covet, but you cannot have what you want. You quarrel and fight. You do not have, because you do not ask God." Jesus promised God would answer those who *continue* to ask, saying in Matthew 7:9–11, " 'Which of you, if his son asks for bread, will give him a stone? Or if he asks for a fish, will give him a snake? If you, then, though you are evil, know how to give good gifts to your children, how much more will your Father in heaven give good gifts to those who ask him!' "

BIRD FEEDER:
Desire is more than a casual craving.

BIRDBATH:
[Jesus said,] " 'Ask and it will be given to you; seek and you will find; knock and the door will be opened to you. For everyone who asks receives; he who seeks finds; and to him who knocks, the door will be opened' " (Matthew 7:7–8).

BIRDHOUSE:
Give me godly pursuits and endurance to keep knocking until the answers come.

FOR THE BIRDS:

Hanging bug catchers are annoying and can chase away birds. Swallows, wrens, and martins in your yard will help control flying insects. Flickers and robins will often take care of anthills and other crawling pests.

Flying in Formation

IN THE spring and fall, giant Canada geese migrate through our area in streamlined V's. Their honking fills the cool air. The lead bird slices the air to make flight easier for the birds directly behind him, and they do the same for the ones behind them. The pattern has a purpose.

Sometimes the front bird tires and falls back and a bird behind will move ahead. They share the responsibility of leadership throughout the journey. When one tires of leading, another is ready to step in—but again, there is order. Birds with seniority in the family lead first. Age and marital status often decide where in the flock a goose is assigned a spot. Order and precision are vital. Each bird gets his or her opportunity at just the right time. They fly at speeds up to seventy miles per hour for great distances with no mishaps or collisions.

The only time I ever saw them in chaos was when someone at the lake shot a gun. Thousands of geese tried to get in the air at the same time, but there was no designated leader. They ran into each other while trying to get away. I've never seen anything like it since. They reminded me of people who suffer catastrophe without a Savior.

When life is settled and without tension, we easily become complacent. If we stop listening for the voice of the Lord, we can miss His call to follow Him when it's time to take flight. The sudden gunfire and the resulting chaos of the geese illustrates the importance of keeping our eyes on Jesus, even while resting in the green pastures into which He led us.

BIRD FEEDER:

A trustworthy leader should be chosen before one is needed.

BIRDBATH:

" 'My sheep listen to my voice; I know them, and they follow me. I give them eternal life, and they shall never perish; no one can snatch them out of my hand' " (John 10:27–28).

BIRDHOUSE:

Lord, You lead me to still waters where my thirst is quenched.

FOR THE BIRDS:

Suet is especially needed for migrating birds. It is inexpensive to buy at the meat counter or grocer. Ask for ground animal fat—the big woodpeckers love it. At least eighty species of North American birds will eat beef kidney suet, including many insect-eating birds that wouldn't normally come to the feeders.

Foot Bath

AFTER I did some major yard work, a hard rain fell for days. Deep ruts spiraled their way through our grass and rainwater filled them to the brim. The dog food in Bandit's outside dish was soaked, so I threw it out into the yard. A few minutes later, an ambitious crow began to gobble down the sopping pellets. As he bounced around getting as many morsels as possible, the claylike mud clung to his feet.

He became so laden with the slimy wet earth that he could barely walk, and flying was out of the question. He hopped clumsily onto the cement patio and began pecking away at his feet. Dirt clumps flew in all directions while he worked to get himself clean. Then he returned to the yard to eat more of the soggy dog food. Within minutes, his mud-covered feet were hindering his progress again. He looked at his feet, the patio, and then a near-by puddle. This time he jumped into the puddle and soaked his feet until they were burden free! Then he returned to finish his breakfast.

Sometimes the drudgery of earning a living can make us feel as though we are dragging our feet through a clinging bog. If we didn't have to eat, we wouldn't have to go back out into the sludge-driven workforce again. But the truth is, "A man can do nothing better than to eat and drink and find satisfaction in his work. This too, I see, is from the hand of God" (Ecclesiastes 2:24). Yet, even with good things in our lives, we can miss life's simplest pleasure if we are shackled by the weight of the work needed to get it.

When the crow came into the fortune of Bandit's spoils, he learned, through trial and error, two ways to rid himself of the burden that kept him from enjoying his work. First he tried tediously to clean himself, only to return immediately to the situation that burdened him again. But crows are known to be intelligent birds, which is evident when he considered his options the second time—patio or puddle?

With effortless soaking in the refreshing water, he easily came clean. The mud simply floated away as he rested in the cleansing power of the puddle. He returned to the water as often as needed while he finished gathering his daily manna.

Likewise, we can *work* at keeping a positive attitude to retain our drive for success and provision. Or we can *rest* in the Living Water of God's truth and let the refreshing power of God's promises keep us full of the zest for life. The crow found splashing in the water to be much easier.

Bird Feeder:

The one who is wise learns from others' mistakes.

Birdbath:

[Jesus said,] " 'Come to me, all you who are weary and burdened, and I will give you rest. Take my yoke upon you and learn from me, for I am gentle and humble in heart, and you will find rest for your souls. For my yoke is easy and my burden is light' "(Matthew 11:28–30).

BIRDHOUSE:
Lord, You lifted me from the miry clay and set my feet upon a rock.
SEE PSALM 40:2

FOR THE BIRDS:
A handful of dog food gives nourishment to larger birds such as crows and woodpeckers.

Goldie

BAM! THE sound of a bird flying into the window is an unhappy sound to bird lovers who keep feeders near their houses. We ran outside to see if this most recent "run-in" was all right. My husband and I found a female goldfinch lying in the lawn chair. Jon picked up the unconscious bird and I encouraged him to gently rub her back. After a few strokes, she blinked and settled into a better position in his cupped hand.

Jon talked to her, and she cocked her head and snuggled in. When he offered her a finger to perch on, she accepted. Looking around the woods and feeling safe, she roosted on his extended digit! A few minutes later, she flew to a nearby branch and preened her feathers. When she was fully recuperated, she went to the feeder for a bite to eat. Looking at the woods and alternately eyeing the window, she finally flew off in the right direction.

Several days later a female goldfinch stayed on the feeders while we moved around the deck. Her trust made me wonder if she was the one who had rested in Jon's hand. We called her Goldie.

Like Goldie, we sometimes fly head-on into a barrier that we didn't see coming. A sudden collision with an unexpected boundary can knock us unconscious. It is during these times that we learn to trust the Father's hand in our lives. Even though we aren't aware of it, He picks us up and warms us in the safety of His presence. When He sees that we are ready to fly, He lifts us up and shows us the blue skies and then waits until we are ready to take off on our own again.

BIRD FEEDER:
Blessed is he whose hope is the Lord his God.

BIRDBATH:

"The LORD gives sight to the blind, the LORD lifts up those who are bowed down, the LORD loves the righteous" (Psalm 146:8).

BIRDHOUSE:

Because I trust You, Lord,
I will continue to feed near Your house.

FOR THE BIRDS:

Plain peanut butter is a high-protein treat for birds. Mix grit or cornmeal with it to keep it from sticking to the outside of a bird's beak. Another good way to serve this snack is to thin it with jelly. Birds love both.

Gone Fishing!

BESIDE A bridge near our home, Jon and I observe American bald eagles from our car. Early one morning we watched as two adult eagles began their breathtaking dance of courtship.

Another day I watched one of these great birds fish for his breakfast. He hovered in midair, watching the murky water below him; then with a sudden drop, he skimmed the water. He missed when a car on the road roared by and broke his concentration. Instead of returning to the river, he settled in a nearby tree, where he fluffed out his feathers and scanned the area. Not wanting to further disturb his dining experience, I left.

Distractions can make me forget about what I had started out to do. While some distractions can be good—such as when a friend encourages me to let housecleaning go another day so we can share an unexpected day together—other things that clutter our lives should be ignored. When I determine to finish something I feel God has inspired me to do, it is amazing how many interruptions suddenly try to divert my focus. I must learn to discern the difference between the sudden splash in the water that shows me where a fish is and the startling noise that makes me want to give up fishing.

BIRD FEEDER:
A clear vision of the prize is not easily forgotten.

BIRDBATH:
"Turn my eyes away from worthless things; preserve my life according to your word" (Psalm 119:37).

BIRDHOUSE:
Lord, I ask for clarity as I focus on Your perfect will.

FOR THE BIRDS:

For a great book of tips on watching North American birds common to your region, look for the National Audubon Society's *The Bird Garden—A comprehensive guide to attracting birds to your backyard throughout the year,* by Stephen W. Kress. Available through DK Publishing, Inc., New York, NY.

Goose Crossing

IN OUR town, if a Canada goose decides to cross the road, he has the right of way. The oncoming driver's first and only warning is when the goose first steps out onto the road.

Several other geese usually play follow-the-leader. They seem to know the law is on their side. They rarely hurry, and sometimes a second group, seeing the traffic is already stopped, will join them. Some drivers inch forward and separate the geese to get past them. The next driver may try to pass on through, but usually when the next goose steps off the curb, it is time to stop again. A blaring honk might move the birds to flight but usually only brings a look of disdain from the geese.

This slow mode of transportation, one webbed foot in front of the other, is often how parent geese move their goslings that cannot fly to better feeding grounds. When the little ones cross, drivers rarely get angry. Babies bring out the best in us—even during rush hour.

BIRD FEEDER:
Good things happen for those who wait on the Lord.

BIRDBATH:
"And therefore the Lord [earnestly] waits [expecting, looking, and longing] to be gracious to you; and therefore He lifts Himself up, that He may have mercy on you *and* show loving-kindness to you. For the Lord is a God of justice. Blessed [happy, fortunate, to be envied] are all those who [earnestly] wait for Him, who expect *and* look *and* long for Him [for His victory, His favor, His love, His peace, His joy, and His matchless, unbroken companionship]!" (Isaiah 30:18 AMPLIFIED).

BIRDHOUSE:
*Thank You for stopping my rush hour
to teach me the benefits of patience.*

FOR THE BIRDS:
To keep ants from climbing your feeder poles
holding liquid food, smear vegetable shorten-
ing on the pole. Use fishing line to hang feeders from the pole if you want to keep large
animals such as squirrels from getting to them.
They can't hang on to the thin thread.

Great Blue Heron

I SLID slowly into the ditch, hoping to get a closer glimpse of the great blue heron. Settling on a rock surrounded by cattails, I waited. A movement in the water caught my eye—and there he stood, watching the water below his spindly legs. In one swift move, the heron caught a fish, stretched his long neck upward, and swallowed! I wondered where the others were, since I had often seen several in this area.

When a semi-trailer went roaring by and backfired, I jumped. So did several herons that were hidden in the cattails around me! When they took off, I was close enough to see their brilliant blue underfeathers and feel the air ripple across my face from their movement. I sat back down on the rock, my heart beating a faster rhythm.

Driving home, I realized the herons had let me enter their secret hiding place. My presence did not alarm them. I couldn't explain their behavior, so I accepted it as a gift from God. I grinned and declared out loud, "Thank You, Lord, for this special blessing today!" I later thought again about the big birds and how I was so involved in looking for them that I almost missed them! Even though surrounded by the birds, I was completely unaware of their presence.

Stories abound about human encounters with angels. Magazines and television shows are filling the media with testimonies of miraculous events as though "heaven on earth" is becoming a more literal expression each year. Figuring out the hype from the hope can be difficult, and seeking an encounter with an angel is discouraged because it takes our focus off God. Yet the Bible clearly tells us in Hebrews 13:2 to extend hospitality to strangers, "for by so doing some people have entertained angels without knowing it."

The importance here is to understand that angels are messengers of God. While we are not to go looking for angels, we are to be sensitive to the fact that God can and will send messages to us through others. We should be alert to the possible places where His messengers might be. I think of the many times I needed an answer from God and how a child, a cashier at the grocery store, or a friend said just the right thing to set my thinking on the right path. Encouragement is often all around us, like herons hiding in the grass.

BIRD FEEDER:
Sometimes the very thing you are looking for has already found you.

BIRDBATH:
"Then they cried to the LORD in their trouble, and he saved them from their distress. He sent forth his word and healed them" (Psalm 107:19–20).

BIRDHOUSE:
*Keep me alert to the messengers
who bring Your Word to me.*

FOR THE BIRDS:
Every serious birder needs a good pair of binoculars. Prices range from $99 to $4,500, and binoculars are offered through trade magazines for bird-watchers and camera stores. Read up on the options before selecting the pair that is right for you; then keep them close by for an extra boost in your favorite pastime.

Hidden Treasure

ONE MORNING I heard an unusual noise outside at the dog food dish. To my surprise, a northern flicker was chasing hungry squirrels away from the bowl by pecking their heads with his beak! He obviously didn't want to share his treasure with anyone. The squirrels scrambled to get away, chirring an angry rebuttal. I watched the industrious bird smash a few nuggets of food on the cement and eat them. Then his day's work began.

He took a piece of dog food in his beak to a nearby tree and stashed it in the trunk. He worked until the dish was empty. Later, I inspected the tree. Dog food was tucked in the bark, up and down the tree. Still on guard, the bird chased me away with a flutter of wings and an angry trill from his throat!

The next morning I watched the squirrels steal every carefully placed morsel from the bark of the tree! By storing the food, the flicker accomplished a good work. Yet, all the bird's hard labor profited him nothing.

Watching the flicker's hidden treasure disappear, I thought about my own work. Does what I do have eternal value, or is it unfruitful like the flicker's hidden treasure?

I reread the parable in Matthew 25:14–28 of the master who gave money to each of three servants. Two of the servants doubled their funds by using it to trade with others and thus returned the increase to their master. The satisfied master then trusted them with even greater opportunities. But the third servant, lacking faith in the master, simply hid the provision, fearing the consequences of owing the master when he returned. Angered by the servant's laziness, the master told the third servant to give his money to the first, who knew how to use it for doing good.

If we have wealth, we are instructed by God in 1 Timothy 6:17 not to put our hope in wealth, "which is so uncertain," but to put our hope in God, "who richly provides us with everything for our enjoyment." The Lord blesses those who share their talents (provisions) with others. He also provides for those who are treated unfairly—even squirrels.

Bird Feeder:
The one who shares enjoys many returns.

Birdbath:
"Command them to do good, to be rich in good deeds, and to be generous and willing to share. In this way they will lay up treasure for themselves as a firm foundation for the coming age, so that they may take hold of the life that is truly life" (1 Timothy 6:18–19).

Birdhouse:
Lord, give me a brave heart
that can give to others and
trust You to provide for us tomorrow.

FOR THE BIRDS:

Apples and oranges delight a host of birds, including flickers and orioles. Even if they seem too old for human consumption, they're still a great treat for the birds!

House Beautiful

MY NEIGHBOR always puts a lovely wreath on her front door. One year she used silk flowers with a flowing raffia bow. Early one morning she heard someone at the door. She looked out, but no one was there. Walking away, she heard the sound again. Stealth seemed to be a good idea, so she went out the side door and peeked around the corner. A female robin was busy building a nest in the curve of the wreath.

Checking on her new tenant the next morning, she was amazed at the little bird's handiwork. The robin had artfully used the raffia ribbon in her construction. The straw was woven in and out in graceful waves along the outside of a mud cup. The nest was so intricately attached to the wreath, my friend worried that using the door might hurt the eggs.

With the tenderness of a grandmother, she pasted a huge note on the door that read,

"Shhh, babies sleeping!

Please use the side door."

From a nearby window she watched the wise mother raise her young. The nest was creative, functional, and protected from wind and rain. This little mother had obviously anchored her family to the right door.

Bird Feeder:

Houses built on rocks are not easily swept away.

Birdbath:

"Then said Jesus unto them again, 'Verily, verily, I say unto you, I am the door of the sheep. . . . I am the door: by me if any man enter in, he shall be saved, and shall go in and out, and find pasture'" (John 10:7, 9 KJV).

BIRDHOUSE:
Lord, I anchor my heart on
Your solid promises.

FOR THE BIRDS:
Purple and house finches (sparrows, too) will often nest in expensive hanging potted plants. Sometimes this damages or kills the plant. An easy solution is to hang a silk plant early in the season somewhere you can keep it up until the babies have grown and gone. They will choose this site early and hopefully leave your more expensive plants alone. (However, this is not a guarantee!)

Hummingbird in the Mist

THE YARD was dry from the brutality of the drought. Cracks were beginning to form in the hard soil, and our grass needed a drink.

The faucet squeaked as I turned on the soaker hose and a gentle mist began to moisten the parched yard. Sitting nearby with a glass of iced tea, I watched the goldfinches and chickadees at the feeders in the unrelenting sunshine. A huge bumblebee bumped into my cheek, backed up, then moved on, buzzing by my ear but missing me the second time.

Droplets of water fastened themselves to our dog cable and glistened in the sunlight. I heard a hum again and turned my head to see if the bee was back. With fascination, I watched as a hummingbird playfully refreshed himself in the mist from the garden sprinkler. Then he landed on the wire and let the gentle spray of water wash over him as he worked his beak over his shimmering emerald feathers.

His little head was soaked, and his tiny feathers stood straight up, making him look like he had a crew cut. Shaking off, he hovered out of range of the water as if to air-dry his small body. Then he nourished himself with the nectar in a nearby feeder.

Seasons without thoughts of God's love can make our hearts feel dry and thirsty. If we let the burdens of our anxieties fill us with dreadful thoughts, we inevitably forget God's truth, and then our hope dries up. We, too, need to rehydrate ourselves when we have been exposed to the heat of disappointments for too long.

As soon as we realize we've lost our "shine," we should watch for an opportunity to play in the rain. If there hasn't been any for a while, we should remember the hummingbird and look around for a garden hose. It's amazing what dancing in a sprinkler can do for a parched perspective and for a hairdo.

Bird Feeder:

In God is the fountain of life; we feast in the abundance of His house and drink in His river of delights (see Psalm 36:8–9).

Birdbath:

"Let us draw near to God with a sincere heart in full assurance of faith, having our hearts sprinkled to cleanse us from a guilty conscience and having our bodies washed with pure water. Let us hold unswervingly to the hope we profess, for he who promised is faithful" (Hebrews 10:22–23).

Birdhouse:

*Lord, Your love rejuvenates me with
its thirst-quenching power.*

For the Birds:

Birds are attracted to running water. If you don't have a fountain birdbath, another good choice is a misting or soaker hose. Turn the water on to a gentle flow in the morning or late afternoon, and then enjoy watching as several kinds of birds play and bathe in the soft mist.

In the Still of the Night

WHEN I was a child, Mom would listen to my prayers, tuck me in with a kiss, and turn out the lights for me. I would lie in my bed and listen to the night sounds through the nearby window as I tried to fall asleep. Outside in the big pine tree an owl asked, "Whooo?"

I wiggled out from under the covers and knelt at the windowsill to look out into the darkness. Between the branches I could see the stars twinkling in the night. With the faith of a little child, I knew heaven was somewhere behind those stars.

I liked leaving the shade up because when the moon was high in the sky, it was a great night-light. Looking into the ebony sky full of stars, I was glad for God's presence in my life.

I scanned the pine branches for the owl, hoping to see his silhouette in the tree. Listening to his night song, I wondered if he was asking who could hear him singing in the night.

Again the owl gently called, "Whooo?"

"Me!" I whispered back to him.

Tired and with very cold feet, I finally climbed back under my covers. The stars and the big bird were my proof that God was real. As my eyes began to droop with sleepiness, I remembered my Sunday school teacher saying, "God never sleeps." I felt safe knowing that God and the owl would be awake to watch over our neighborhood in the still of the night.

Evening still echoes the calls of the owl in our woods. Many nights find me barefooted and looking into the vast night sky, hoping to catch a glimpse of this nocturnal bird. The stars continue to twinkle from where God placed them to light up the night—and it is good.

In those sweet nights of my childhood, I was just becoming aware of the awesome presence of God in my life. I understand what David may have felt when he wrote of God in Psalm 16:11, "You have made known to me the path of life; you will fill me with joy in your presence, with eternal pleasures at your right hand."

Now when I hear the owl calling, I like to think he wonders, "Who will praise God for His great and wonderful works?"

And I still whisper in response, "Me!"

BIRD FEEDER:
"Come and see what God has done, how awesome his works in man's behalf!" (Psalm 66:5).

BIRDBATH:
"At midnight I will rise to give thanks to You because of Your righteous ordinances" (Psalm 119:62 AMPLIFIED).

BIRDHOUSE:
My heart is at rest in Your presence, Lord.
(see 1 John 3:19)

FOR THE BIRDS:
Owls will nest in an open-ended box mounted at a 45° angle about 10' to 30' up from the ground. Make the base 9" square and drill

holes in the bottom to let moisture drain out. Make two sides that are 9" x 30", a base that is 10½" x 30", and a roof that is 10½" by 36". The extra length provides an overhang to protect the opening from rain. Drill five holes in a 2¾" x 27½" mounting batten: three to screw the batten to the house at a 45° angle, with the two holes at each end attaching the box to the tree. Spread sawdust or peat in the bottom of the nest to create an inviting cavity for owls to raise their young.

Is It Spring Yet?

EACH YEAR the sweet southern breezes melt the ice and snow. The rains and warmer temperatures turn the grass green. Crocuses and tulips break through the ground. For me, it is spring when all the birds come home.

My spring vigil begins with the robins, which are usually the first to arrive. I watch as the goldfinches that braved our cold temperatures by staying here molt their winter disguise and turn bright yellow. Then come the orioles, warblers, hummingbirds, cedar waxwings, indigo buntings, bluebirds, purple martins, tree swallows, and scarlet tanagers. White pelicans rest on the nearby lake in their long migration north. I scan the marshlands for the egrets and finally the great blue herons.

As I watch the return of the birds, each arrival is a comfort to me that the seasons will continue just as God promised. Genesis 8:22 says, "As long as the earth endures, seedtime and harvest, cold and heat, summer and winter, day and night will never cease."

We refer to the migration of birds as a behavior of their natural instincts. They just seem to know which direction to go and when they should begin their trip. We can understand how their instinct operates by comparing it to our own natural propensity for knowing right from wrong. We have peace when we do the right thing and unrest when we react contrary to God's better design for us.

A personal application of Romans 1:19 (AMPLIFIED) says, "For that which is known about God is evident to [us] *and* made plain in [our] inner consciousness, because God [Himself] has shown it to [us]. Verse 20 explains, "For ever since the creation of the world His invisible nature *and* attributes, that is, His eternal power and divinity, have been made intelligible *and* clearly discernible in *and* through the things that have been made [His handiworks]."

The migration of the birds bears testimony that God has a plan for us. The Word of God continues to make clear in Romans 1:20–21 that we are without excuse, altogether without any defense or justification if we do not recognize the Lord as God, and honor Him and give Him thanks.

The difference between the birds and we humans is that we have been given the power of choice to follow God or not. We can ignore that internal compass of consciousness and go our own way. But if we follow Jesus, who is the way to the Father, He promises to lead us as a shepherd to green pastures and still waters where we can be refreshed and restored (Psalm 23). Surely goodness, mercy, and unfailing love follow those who choose to stay in the presence of God.

BIRD FEEDER:
When in doubt, do what love would do.

BIRDBATH:
"Heaven and earth will pass away, but my words will never pass away" (Matthew 24:35).

BIRDHOUSE:

*Lord, the heavens declare Your glory
and the earth shows Your handiwork.*

FOR THE BIRDS:

Sprinkle millet on the ground for brown-headed cowbirds, mourning doves, sparrows, and juncos that prefer feeding on the ground. If you see quail, the curve-billed thrasher, or the Steller's jay, throw some millet on the ground for them, too. The blue jay, junco, black-capped chickadee, and mourning doves will help clean up milo, even though they prefer millet.

Letting Go

FEARLESS, OUR pet raccoon, was our wild little friend who came to us as a baby needing food, shelter, and love. At three years old, he began to reject us. Becoming aggressive and pacing his kennel, he snarled at us and no longer reached up to be held. He let us know through his unruly behavior that it was time to return him to his natural habitat.

We learned of a place in the backwaters of the Mississippi River about ninety minutes away where we could take him deep into the woods beside a small stream and set him free. With Fearless in the pet carrier, we thrashed through nettles and weeds more than six feet tall. The thick underbrush tripped us.

Huge trees seemed to stand watch as we

entered deeper into the forest. The stream bubbled over rocks, and a downed tree rested across the water. Birdsong surrounded us even in the deep, thick woods. We heard duck calls and saw small fish in the glistening stream. Raspberry bushes were in full bloom. This was the right place—a raccoon's paradise.

We watched Fearless as he peeked out of the carrier and took his first steps into freedom. He sniffed the air and touched the water before venturing into it, and then he paddled and floated immediately. Climbing a tree was easy for him, though coming down was a bit harder. We could see that he would make it on his own.

Fearless did all the things a wild raccoon should: He could swim, eat minnows and crunchy things from the stream, and climb to safety in a tree. After looking at us one more time as if to say "good-bye," he disappeared in the tall weeds. We never saw him again. Turning to leave, I asked God to protect him.

A soft whooshing sound got my attention. A great blue heron settled onto the small log and blinked his eye at me. He was close, less than four feet away from me, and fully aware of my presence. He blinked once more and then gazed into the water. It was time for us to go, time for Fearless to be free, time for the heron to fish for his lunch.

Following the stream out of the woods, we came to where spring water flowed out from behind a rock. Splashing in and out of its gentle flow was an indigo bunting, scarlet tanager, and a yellow warbler. I walked up to the natural fountain and put my hands in the cold water while the birds darted in and out around me.

We knew we were doing the right thing, but it was still hard. I walked away feeling we had done the best we could for a little raccoon. And I was comforted by the birds that God sent to welcome Fearless to his new home.

BIRD FEEDER:
Doing the right thing often requires sacrifice.

BIRDBATH:
"For every beast of the forest is Mine, *and* the cattle upon a thousand hills *or* upon the mountains where thousands are. I know *and* am

acquainted with all the birds of the mountains, and the wild animals of the field are Mine *and* are with Me, in My mind" (Psalm 50:10–11 AMPLIFIED).

BIRDHOUSE:

Give me wisdom to know when it is time to embrace and time to refrain from embracing.

FOR THE BIRDS:

To keep raccoons, possums, and other wild animals from eating all your seed, leave leftovers for them. They love old bread, muffins, cookies, pasta—almost everything. Meat products attract flies and should only be left when you know it will be eaten that night. Dried corn also helps to keep the squirrels off the feeders—but not entirely.

Love Song

ONE SPRING I heard a lovely song in the woods. The sweet melody came from high in an ironwood tree. I searched the budding branches for the source of the singer. The only bird in the tree was a feisty blue jay that seemed to find my presence a nuisance. He squawked and I moved a few feet away, hoping the other bird would start singing again.

Sitting at the picnic table, I waited. In a few moments the melodious song resounded from the limbs of the same tree. I was certain the only bird there was that noisy old jay. Then I saw him open his mouth in song and release lovely sounds from his throat. Delight followed my surprise. He was pouring on the charm, hoping some lady jay would appreciate his love song! Throughout the day he kept the song soft and romantic.

When I saw another bird fly to him later that day, I grinned with hopes that the flirty bird had found his mate. That evening their coarse, raspy calls filled the air as they conversed—so much for the gentle wooing earlier today!

Isn't that just like romance? At first, we put on our best clothes, smile, and attitude. We draw the one we love in by our wooing; we put effort into listening and caring. Then as we take each other for granted, our love song becomes rusty from a lack of use.

God never stops wooing us to a relationship with Him. He so loves us that He sent His only begotten Son to demonstrate to us what love really is. And His Son, Jesus, loved us so much that He let us mock Him, spit on Him, and even beat Him, yet He still gave Himself as a sacrifice for the sins that kept us from knowing God as our Father.

Matthew, Mark, Luke, and John knew Jesus and witnessed His character both before and after He was crucified (see Acts 1:3). They testify that Jesus is patient, kind, and always mediating with God for our lives. Jesus is never boastful, proud, rude, or self-seeking. He is not easily angered and certainly keeps no record of wrongs. He never delights in evil but always rejoices with the truth. He always protects, always trusts, always hopes, and always perseveres for us.

These attributes of love that Jesus demonstrates perfectly toward us are listed in 1 Corinthians 13:4–13, and we can love others this same way if we invite Christ to live in us. When we learn to react to people the way Jesus would react to them, both the woods and the world will be filled with a sweet melody.

BIRD FEEDER:
People don't care how much we know until they know how much we care.

BIRDBATH:
"And so faith, hope, love abide [faith—conviction and belief respecting man's relation to God and divine things; hope—joyful and confident expectation of eternal salvation; love—

true affection for God and man, growing out of God's love for and in us], these three; but the greatest of these is love" (1 Corinthians 13:13 AMPLIFIED).

BIRDHOUSE:
God, live in my heart and love others through my words and deeds.

FOR THE BIRDS:
Birdseed can spoil or become infested with moths. If possible, keep surplus seed in the freezer. The frozen food thaws quickly for the birds' consumption and the freezing keeps it fresh.

Making Mud

SPRING BUDDED everywhere. The lilac bushes were bursting open, the warm breeze whispered hope to the heart, tulips were pushing through the hard ground, and the robins were back. But no rain came, and it looked like another year of drought.

I watered the tulips and filled the birdbaths. Tired birds of all kinds came for the fresh water. From my kitchen window, I watched a young female robin begin building her nest. Robins use mud to hold sticks together in their nest. But there was no mud. So, this industrious bird flew to the birdbath and gathered a tiny bit of water in her mouth. From there she flew to a bare piece of ground on the edge of the lawn. She pounded the water with her beak into the hard dirt. She then used that tiny bit of mud to cement one twig to another.

Her labors and the remaining task before her overwhelmed my heart. After watching her make a dozen trips, I helped her out. I turned the garden hose on and made a little puddle in the dirt for her. I also cleaned and refilled the now muddy birdbath.

Back in the kitchen, I peeked out to see if she understood the opportunity before her. She tipped her head back and belted out a sweet note of song before returning to her task. By the end of the day, her nest was complete, finished off with a long piece of orange ribbon she found somewhere. Her simple decoration blew gracefully in the gentle breeze.

I later found two tiny pieces of aqua eggshells on the ground and heard her babies peeping from the security of the nest. I knew I had helped them, too. When we do a good deed, we sometimes never see the generations that are blessed by the work of our hands.

The robin instinctively knew that she needed something stronger than twigs to hold her home together so she could nurture her family. We need something strong to keep our homes together, too. For us, loving someone may come easily, but it is commitment that holds our relationships together. Keeping a promise is hard work and sometimes as glamorous as making mud, but commitment brings a fruitful reward.

BIRD FEEDER:
When is the last time you made mud pies with someone?

BIRDBATH:
"Do not withhold good from those who deserve it, when it is in your power to act" (Proverbs 3:27).

BIRDHOUSE:
Lord, teach me to use my hands and my words to build up my home.

FOR THE BIRDS:
While watering flowers, rinse the outside of liquid feeders daily with the garden hose to

keep the sugary water from attracting bees and wasps. The sting of a wasp or hornet can kill a hummingbird. Other birds that stop for a drink often help the hummers out. The downy woodpecker drinks sugar water and doesn't mind chasing away the wasps and hornets. Chickadees will also join these birds for a drink.

"Morning" Doves

GRANDMA AND I sat on the steps outside her apartment. She was teaching me to sweep the sidewalk, something she did most mornings in hopeful anticipation of visitors. The soft song of the brown doves resting on the telephone wires floated on the morning air. The sound comforted me. Grandpa was gone, but they told me heaven welcomed him. My nine-year-old heart only knew I missed him and it hurt.

"Grandma, what kind of birds are those?" I asked.

"Mourning doves," she replied.

"Because they sing in the morning?" I asked.

Grandma smiled, "No, Child, they get their name from their sad song."

Dissatisfied with her answer, I asked,

"Grandma, I like their songs. Can I call them the *morning* doves?"

"Yes," she agreed.

I understand why Jesus welcomed children to Him; they perceive the brighter side of life and God. Speaking of children, Jesus once said, " 'I tell you the truth, anyone who will not receive the kingdom of God like a little child will never enter it' " (Luke 18:17).

Grown-ups often recognize God as the Creator of our universe, while a child might know Him better as their loving heavenly Father. Some see Jesus as a good man and teacher, yet others know Him as the Son of God. Both views alone are incomplete, for Jesus stripped Himself of His divine privileges to become a man, but He was still God, possessing the fullness of all the attributes that make God who He is (see Philippians 2:6–7 and John 1:14 AMPLIFIED). God loves us with the passion of a father, but that is why He sometimes disciplines us in love. In every case, one view without the other is out of balance and clouds the truth, just as mature reasoning without childlike faith misses God's best for us.

As a child, it was not difficult for me to believe that Grandpa was in heaven, but it was hard to believe that the doves were sad when their songs hummed with contentment. My heart ached, but their song offered consolation. Today, the fluttering of their wings soothes like the rhythmic swing of Grandma's broom as she made ready for a new day full of promise, and their sweet song reminds me to look for the brighter side of difficult truths.

BIRD FEEDER:

"For His anger is but for a moment, his favor is for life; weeping may endure for a night, but joy comes in the morning" (Psalm 30:5 NKJV).

BIRDBATH:

"But our citizenship is in heaven. And we eagerly await a Savior from there, the Lord Jesus Christ, who, by the power that enables him to bring everything under his control, will transform our lowly bodies so that they will be like his glorious body" (Philippians 3:20–21).

BIRDHOUSE:
Each new morning, Lord,
I will settle into the hope of
Your coming again.

FOR THE BIRDS:

The next time you see mourning doves in your yard, open the door and listen to the whistling of their wings as they fly away. It sounds like a squeaky hinge on an old garden gate—yet another wonder of God's creation.

Out of
the Nest

WALKING IN our yard one afternoon, I was bombarded by a female robin! I ducked while she dove and swooped. Looking down at my feet, I saw a baby robin scurry out of the way. Its tiny breast was a downy patch of brown spots. Backing away, I looked up; high in the branches was the nest with two other little ones peeking out. The bird in the brambles was too young to be out of the nest, but it was too high for me to help return him to safety.

At sunset I watched the mother robin shoo her baby back into the underbrush before she returned to the nest. I prayed the Lord would protect the one hidden in the woods.

Early the next morning, the baby robin was out of hiding. The mother divided her time between the little ones above and the lonely one below. She scolded her grounded baby when he got too far away. He responded by scurrying for cover. I watched this routine for four days. On the fifth morning, the mother sat on the ground surrounded by three hungry youngsters. I watched their flight practice—they flew when she chased them!

Like the baby robin, we can get too close to the edge and fall away from God's plan for us. For a time we may even prefer the prickly underbrush instead of the security of God's blessings. When confronted with our stubbornness, we often run for a hiding place in the thorns—even when He is clearly offering the sweet shelter of His wings.

If we have fallen out of the nest and away from God's perfect will for our lives, we only need to listen for His voice to lead us back to the shelter of His wings—the place of perfect peace. When we come to Him, He will faithfully watch over us and protect us while we learn to use our own wings.

BIRD FEEDER:
Obedience will keep us in the safety of the nest so we won't get caught in dark dangers of the brush.

BIRDBATH:
"But I call to God, and the LORD saves me" (Psalm 55:16).

BIRDHOUSE:
*Thank You for forgiving me when
my curiosity causes me
to fall from Your plan.*

FOR THE BIRDS:
Leave areas of fall leaf litter under shrubs or other areas where grass doesn't grow in your yard for birds such as robins and brown thrashers that forage through them for insects.

Ringo

IN THE '70s, when Beatlemania invaded the airwaves, we had our own personal drummer. Every day a redheaded woodpecker we called Ringo sat on the edge of an empty oil drum. Suddenly he would beat the rusted metal. The sound reverberated through the neighborhood. He didn't seem to mind us watching him from a close proximity, and he apparently could not even hear our approach. I often worried he would get a headache or even suffer brain damage! Later I learned God created all woodpeckers with special shock absorbers in their heads.

Sometimes our endeavors feel as futile as Ringo's attempts to find nourishment in an empty oil drum. We beat our heads against walls, but they still don't move. We even wonder why God doesn't stop us from our own tirade of stubborn pursuits; but the Bible tells that He formed each of us with great care, and we are never hidden from Him or His concern. Our problem is not the whereabouts of God, for even though He is standing right next to us, we only focus on the contents of that which has been sealed up from our inspection.

If we are trusting God, the very things that seem so unobtainable might not even be good for us. Sometimes it is grace that keeps us from the thing we want. But we can always find God when we need Him. He is always watching us, even when we're not paying attention to Him. Psalm 139:7–10, 13–14, 16–18 says:

> *Where can I go from your Spirit?*
> *Where can I flee from your presence? If I*
> *go up to the heavens, you are there; if I*
> *make my bed in the depths, you are*
> *there. If I rise on the wings of the dawn,*
> *if I settle on the far side of the sea, even*
> *there your hand will guide me, your*
> *right hand will hold me fast.*
>
> *For you created my inmost being;*
> *you knit me together in my mother's*
> *womb. I praise you because I am fear-*
> *fully and wonderfully made; your works*

are wonderful, I know that full well.

*All the days ordained for me were
written in your book before one of them
came to be. How precious to me are your
thoughts, O God! How vast is the sum of
them! Were I to count them, they would
outnumber the grains of sand. When I
awake, I am still with you."*

Ringo never realized we were standing near
him or that we thought of him every time we
heard him potentially hurting himself. Like
Ringo's built-in shock absorber, God has given
us amazing bodies resistant to the undue stress
of the world in which we live. He gave us able
minds to understand His Word and souls capable of responding to His call. He also gave us
an inner sense of awareness of His presence,
even a desire to be near Him. His salvation
gives us a way of escape from the futility of life.
If we will draw near to Him, even when we are
feeling frustrated by unfruitful works, He promises to draw near to us.

BIRD FEEDER:
If a door doesn't open, it may be locked for a good reason.

BIRDBATH:
"Wait for the LORD; be strong and take heart and wait for the LORD" (Psalm 27:14).

BIRDHOUSE:
"I am still confident of this:
I will see the goodness of the LORD
in the land of the living."

PSALM 27:13

FOR THE BIRDS:
Melt suet until it is a thick liquid; then mix in peanut butter, nuts, cereal, and seeds to make your own suet cake. Line muffin cups with wax paper and spoon the warm mixture in. When it is cool, wrap the wax paper around

the suet and put the cakes in freezer bags. Freezing keeps it fresh and makes it easier to handle when you take it outside.

Same Time Next Year

FOR THREE years a pair of tree swallows returned to the nest they built under our deck. They anchored the mud and twig bowl on a beam outside our basement window—the perfect place for watching them! With each spring arrival, they diligently fixed the damage winter had done to their summer home.

After a few weeks of busy work, they slowed down. Sitting on their remodeled nest or perched in a nearby tree, they watched and waited. Other birds sometimes tried to destroy their home, so they guarded the empty nest with diligence. In the evenings they swooped through the air to catch the bugs so abundant in our woods. Eventually the female sat on the nest.

I closed the blinds partway, leaving only room for a peek so my movements would not disturb them. Each year they hatched two young babies, which filled the mud nest to capacity in a short time. Both parents fed and watched over the babies. As nighttime approached, Mama settled in, making sure the babies were under her wings, while Papa stood guard on the beam above.

The swallows carefully considered their building site. Safe placement of the nest was part of their survival. They secured a strong foundation with protection from the elements and predators. Our spiritual life depends on the same careful selection. Where we decide to place our faith is the foundation of our beliefs. All building takes time and effort, but not all buildings last. Because longevity requires a firm foundation, finding a solid footing should be foremost in our plans.

Jesus said, " 'The one who hears my words and does not put them into practice is like a man who built a house on the ground without a foundation. The moment the torrent struck that house, it collapsed and its destruction was complete' " (Luke 6:49).

But if we both hear and do what Jesus

taught, He says we will be " 'like a man building a house, who dug down deep and laid the
foundation on rock. When a flood came, the
torrent struck that house but could not shake
it, because it was well built' " (Luke 6:48).

The swallows know that they must collect
new materials to rebuild their home after the
brutality of winter storms. There will be new
storms that will try to rage against us, but God
has new mercies to show us each day. We, too,
must continue to rebuild our faith by storing
up the treasure of God's Word in our hearts
and by using our faith while waiting to see
answers to our prayers.

BIRD FEEDER:
When the storms of life hit, even those living
on the beach move inland to solid ground.

BIRDBATH:
"Command them to do good, to be rich in
good deeds, and to be generous and willing to
share. In this way they will lay up treasure for

themselves as a firm foundation for the coming age, so that they may take hold of the life that is truly life" (1 Timothy 6:18–19).

BIRDHOUSE:

*Lord, You are my fortress
and the rock in
whom I take refuge.*

SEE PSALM 94:22

FOR THE BIRDS:

Tree swallows will nest in a box house that has a base of 5" x 5" with an opening of 1". The hole should be 5" from the bottom of the nest.

Scout

A WHISTLE and banging at the kitchen window interrupted my quiet time. Outside, a Baltimore oriole perched on the window ledge, looking for his favorite treat in the spot I usually put jelly when the orioles come. I wondered if this was the same bird that had visited me last year. How else would he have known where the jelly had been? I filled the dish to the top with his favorite flavor—grape. As I stepped outside, he flew to a nearby branch, whistling cheerfully. We almost collided when I turned to hurry away and he flew straight to the bowl now suspended on a string.

For a week, he was the only oriole in the yard, and I wondered if he was the one who was blazing the trail for the others to follow. I called him Scout. I talked to him as he sat unafraid on the other side of the screen, eating jelly and preening his bright orange and black feathers. Within a few days, the yard was filled with the whistling call of other orioles. Keeping the jelly dishes full was a daily ritual. If I didn't, Scout banged on the window with his beak to remind me.

Waiting for Scout to return last spring, I thought of how much courage it takes to be a forerunner for others. I once heard of a young man named Steve, who served the United States in the Vietnam War. He told of how his troop had to walk through dangerous minefields. Each soldier was to take his turn being the point man, but few had the nerve to withstand the pressure. When Steve's turn came, he prayed in the name of Jesus for God to lead them safely through the dangerous fields. The other men had so much confidence in Steve's God that they asked him to continue to lead them with his faith, to which he bravely agreed. They all returned home safely at the end of the war.

Steve wasn't the one who knew where the mines were buried, but he had a personal relationship with the One who did know where they were hidden. Steve was simply following Jesus, but he found that others gratefully followed him to the Prize.

Bird Feeder:
"The fear of the LORD is the beginning of wisdom; all who follow his precepts have good understanding" (Psalm 111:10).

Birdbath:
"But Christ is faithful as a son over God's house. And we are his house, if we hold on to our courage and the hope of which we boast" (Hebrews 3:6).

Birdhouse:
I sought You, Lord,
and You answered me;
You delivered me from all my fears.

SEE PSALM 34:4

For the Birds:
Orioles love grape jelly! Chickadees, cardinals, warblers, downy woodpeckers, and nuthatches all take their turns for a bite of this sweet delicacy.

Stolen Fish

THE DOLPHIN pool at the park was crowded with tourists. I waited in line for the fish stand to open. The sign at the window warned customers to protect their purchases from the seagulls. After buying three containers of small silver fish, I stacked them carefully in one hand and covered them with the other.

Immediately after I stepped away from the shelter of the building, they attacked. One gull swooped at my face; when I moved my hand to protect myself, another knocked the containers to the ground. Their assault seemed well rehearsed. The vendor and many visitors heard my scream. The gull diving for my face had struck my hand, and it was bleeding. I washed my hands at a nearby faucet and the fish vendor brought three more containers to me. I made it safely to the pool where our nephews and niece were waiting to feed the dolphins. The dolphins got the fish this time, and one even begged to have his tummy scratched, to which we all obliged him.

Stepping back, I watched the gulls hovering over the fish shack. The birds learned that if they wanted to eat, they had to go where the fish were, either to water or human hands. They weren't concerned with where they had to go to catch fish; they just by nature loved to fish. The most opportune time to find fish at this park was when the dolphins were being fed.

Jesus fished for people who felt alienated from God. He described His mission to some fishermen as a desire to fish for lost souls; and if they would follow Him, He promised to make them "fishers of men" (see Mark 1:16–20). Jesus knew they had to go where the people were, because lost people can't find the way out of their own entrapment. So, He went to the highways and byways to seek and to save those who needed direction back to His Father.

Jesus was often criticized by the religious leaders of His day for being with people who were known for breaking God's laws. "On hearing this, Jesus said, 'It is not the healthy who need a doctor, but the sick. But go and learn what this means: "I desire mercy, not sacrifice." For I have not come to call the righteous, but sinners' " (Matthew 9:12–13).

Knowing that His time on earth would be brief, He taught twelve men to share the Good News that God has made a way for us to come back to Him through trusting Jesus. They were to teach more disciples to spread the message, and somehow, over the past two thousand years, this love for fishing for lost souls has continued to be passed on to each new generation. After all, someone found us when we were lost and hungry for God. Because Jesus knew where to find His "fish," we, too, have been caught in His net of love.

BIRD FEEDER:
Bait works because it satisfies a need.

BIRDBATH:
"He [Jesus] stood up to read. . . . He found the

place where it is written: 'The Spirit of the Lord is on me, because he has anointed me to preach good news to the poor. He has sent me to proclaim freedom for the prisoners and recovery of sight for the blind, to release the oppressed, to proclaim the year of the Lord's favor.'

"Then he rolled up the scroll. . . . The eyes of everyone in the synagogue were fastened on him, and he began by saying to them, 'Today this scripture is fulfilled in your hearing'" (Luke 4:16–21).

BIRDHOUSE:
I have heard the Good News and am free to enjoy the Lord's favor.

FOR THE BIRDS:
Seagulls and pelicans often follow inland rivers and settle on lakes during their migratory flights. For a taste of coastal birding, check your regional bird calendars to see when these seawater birds might be passing through your state. Even Oklahoma has a pelican festival in the fall!

The Brown Thrashers

I WATCHED a rusty-brown thrasher and his mate carry twigs and grass into the messy branches of a brush pile nearby. They stopped occasionally to watch me with their bright yellow eyes as I cleaned my garden. A couple of days later, the male sat on a branch above the nesting spot while the female rested in the twig cup. She moved and revealed five tiny eggs.

One warm morning while planting seeds, I heard a tiny pecking sound. The thrashers watched from above the nest. I moved closer and saw a recently hatched baby thrasher. Others were working to release themselves from their protective shells. Soon the nest was filled with the demanding cries of baby birds.

The next morning, the brush pile was

silent. The nest was empty. I sat on the edge of my flowerbed staring at the tiny brown cup tucked in the branches. An old hurt surfaced unexpectedly. My friend Pam and her husband Chuck have four living children and two tiny ones in heaven. Jenna and Ryan were born only to live a few hours.

The missing birds caused me to finally face the death of two children whose tender smiles I would not see and giggles I would not hear. Pam and Chuck grieved deeply, yet they never quit trusting God. But how?

I looked into the clear blue sky and asked out loud, "Why, God?" He was silent. Life went on around me as the tree swallows dipped and dove to catch insects. A spider worked on a lace web between two blossoms. Hummingbirds sipped sugar water from their feeder. Butterflies and bees worked the flowers for nectar. Still I waited for an answer.

A verse I learned a long time before from Proverbs 3:5 was whispered to my heart, "Trust in the LORD with all your heart and lean not on your own understanding." I put my head on my knees and sobbed. "But it doesn't make sense, Lord. I just don't get it," I whispered.

A verse came to mind from John 14:1: " 'Do

not let your hearts be troubled. Trust in God; trust also in me.' " Jesus had used this verse to comfort His disciples as He told them of heaven. He knew He would be leaving them; and in His concern for them, He promised them a gift, a Comforter—His Spirit. I felt this deep truth fill my soul as God's Holy Spirit was comforting my heart. I was hearing the still small voice of God as He spoke to me through His Word.

Relying on the hope of heaven, the truth of God's Word, and the comfort of the Holy Spirit, Pam and Chuck survived the grief they felt. They trusted God even when their loss hurt more than any other human experience. Clinging to His promises, they continued to live for God, even when circumstances didn't make sense.

I stood up, stiff, sunburned, and sweat soaked. "Okay, Lord, I trust You." With the decision made, I walked away from the empty nest.

BIRDBATH:

"What is seen is temporary, but what is unseen is eternal" (2 Corinthians 4:18).

BIRD FEEDER:

"If you call out for insight and cry aloud for understanding, and if you look for it as for silver and search for it as for hidden treasure, then you will understand the fear of the LORD and find the knowledge of God" (Proverbs 2:3–5).

BIRDHOUSE:

Lord, as I trust in You
I am filled with peace,
and You cause my heart
to overflow with hope.

SEE ROMANS 15:13

For the Birds:

Hummingbirds are attracted to brightly colored tubular flowers. Plant a variety of flowers that will keep your garden blooming from spring to fall. Hollyhock, butterfly bush, cardinal flowers, larkspur, morning glory, petunias, phlox, trumpet vines, salvia, zinnias, and lantanas are easy to grow, heat-resistant flowers that will keep birds and butterflies visiting your yard.

The Bluebirds

WHILE WEEDING around the wild rose, I saw a bluebird fly into a house that my husband had put up the previous fall. Sparrows had already inspected this plain wood house on the metal pole in my garden, but I really hoped the shy blue and orange birds would live there. They did.

All spring the birds and I worked the garden together. I was in charge of weeds while they were my pest control team. I worked one section of the large flowerbed; the birds hunted for grubs, bugs, and moths for their young. The bees joined us in working the coneflower, daisy, blanket flower, flax, poppy, yarrow, wild rose, and black-eyed Susan blossoms. I sometimes sat on the bench and the male bluebird sat on a nearby branch. Break time!

The shy birds didn't mind my presence, singing, or praying out loud. For some reason, they trusted me. Together we enjoyed our mini-prairie of blossoms. My garden duties that summer did more than keep the garden free of weeds. Prayer weeded out my worries, sorrows, and chaos. Peace, comfort, and joy were encouraged to bloom. I left each day with an aching and sweating body, but my soul was renewed.

Surrounded by God's flowers and the acceptance of the gentle birds, I found that God had touched my life and strengthened my faith. While the bluebirds and I worked the garden, the flowers did what they do best—they grew. So did I.

BIRD FEEDER:
Many hands make light work, and extra wings help, too.

BIRDBATH:

" 'Therefore I tell you, do not worry about your life, what you will eat or drink; or about your body, what you will wear. . . . Look at the birds of the air; they do not sow or reap or store away in barns, and yet your heavenly Father feeds them. Are you not much more valuable than they? Who of you by worrying can add a single hour to his life? . . . See how the lilies of the field grow. They do not labor or spin. . . . If that is how God clothes the grass of the field, which is here today and tomorrow is thrown into the fire, will he not much more clothe you, O you of little faith?' " (Matthew 6:25–28, 30).

BIRDHOUSE:

Lord, I have learned to
lay aside my worries
and put my trust in You.

FOR THE BIRDS:

Bluebird houses are available at most garden supply stores. They need a floor area that is 4" x 4" with an entrance 8" from the bottom that is $1^3/_8$" wide. Mount the house on a pole from 3' to 6' above the ground within 50' of a tree, fence, or other appropriate perch where the male can watch the opening of the hole when his family is nesting.

The Cold Snap

MY GRANDMA Pater lived alone in a tiny country house with four rooms and a porch. Outside she had a big yard and a small orchard filled with golden plum trees. The old pump on her farm had the coldest water I had ever tasted. She didn't have pets, but sometimes for company and recreation she raised a few geese or sheep.

Staying overnight meant sleeping in her kitchen/living room on the hide-a-bed. Usually she woke me up by tickling me with a long pheasant feather, but one morning loud peeps brought me suddenly out of a deep sleep. The sound came from a box by the big heater. Inside were little yellow puffs of down. Because the weather had turned cold and icy in the night, Grandma had gathered the goslings and brought them indoors. The parent birds would survive the cold snap, but she knew the little ones needed this extra protection.

Most mornings Grandma fried eggs with lacy whites and hard yolks for me. But that morning she mixed mash and fed the yellow peeping babies, instead. The silly geese walked in their food, splashed in the water, and bickered with each other. When the more aggressive ones had eaten, Grandma picked them up and put them in a clean box, giving the others a chance. Soon all the babies made the transition and were napping.

The weather warmed up after a couple of days, and Grandma carried the growing geese back outside. I worried the mother geese would not take their babies back, but Grandma's protection seemed to have worked for everyone when the time of crisis was over. The mothers welcomed their goslings back with honks, and soon they were all pecking at the food and mash. Their reunion was uncomplicated.

We sometimes need a place of refuge when our young faith lacks experience in crisis management. God gently cares for us as my loving grandmother cared for the goslings. The storms in our life can rage, but we are warmed by His love. Although His Word is near to strengthen us, many of us just grovel in it like goslings in the mash without knowing how to ingest it and grow. But God does not hurry us. He lets us splash unknowingly in His truth and bicker in the midst of blessing, but He patiently keeps offering His grace to us until it is safe to set us back outside to face the elements again.

BIRD FEEDER:
Even though we don't completely understand God's Word, it is good to wallow in it until we do.

BIRDBATH:
"He will cover you with his feathers, and under his wings you will find refuge; his faithfulness will be your shield and rampart" (Psalm 91:4).

BIRDHOUSE:

*I shall remain stable and fixed
under the shadow of Your wing,
whose power no foe can withstand.*

SEE PSALM 91:1

FOR THE BIRDS:

Birds need water in the winter, too. A heater can be purchased for the birdbath to keep water from freezing. Basins of water buried to ground level will not freeze as quickly as aboveground basins, since the earth stays close to 40° even when air temperatures drop to freezing.

The Cowbird

A FAMILY of cardinals came to the feeders late one afternoon. The babies had tufts of fluff mixed in with their new feathers. There were four baby birds; three were red and one was two-toned brown. The baby cowbird's mother had abandoned her egg (a common cowbird practice) in the cardinal's nest when they weren't looking. The faithful redbirds sat on the strange egg and fed the young two-toned brown bird, never questioning his right to be there, knowing his survival depended on what they could give him.

Already bigger than his adoptive parents, he demanded the lion's share of their attention. But the wise parents kept track of each bite their young were given and taught them all to eat. The birds left together and headed back to a crowded nest. The next morning the family returned. The parents gave each of their crew a bite, then waited for their young to feed themselves. The adults gently touched the younger birds' beaks, including the cowbird's. Not one of the cardinals was uncomfortable with the bigger bird, and they accepted him as their own. He was family!

All summer a group of three young cardinals chased and played at the feeders, carefully watched by a young cowbird. Sleek feathers soon replaced the fluff. The young drop-off and his nest mates were ready to live as adult birds in the woods. One day, another bird wearing the same shades of brown showed up at the feeder and left with the two-toned brown "redbird."

Like the cowbird to the cardinals, we are God's adopted children through our faith in Jesus Christ. Though Jesus came as the promised Savior to the Jewish people, God accepted all those who received Jesus as their Lord. God does not look at the color of our "feathers" but at the faith in our hearts. Those who put their hope in the risen Christ are made joint-heirs to all the provisions made for God's royal family. He feeds us His Word, warms us with His promises, and nurtures us to maturity in His perfect plan.

BIRD FEEDER:
Mercy forgives the punishment deserved; grace gives the blessing unearned.

BIRDBATH:
"He [Jesus] came to that which was his own, but his own did not receive him. Yet to all who received him, to those who believed in his name, he gave the right to become children of God" (John 1:11–12).

BIRDHOUSE:
Thank You, Father, for Your mercy and grace.

FOR THE BIRDS:
Many birds enjoy peanut butter. A good way to serve it is to smear it onto a pinecone, then

roll it in mixed birdseed. Tie a string to the top and hang the cone from a tree or pole. Peanuts in the shells are a welcome treat for blue jays, squirrels, and woodpeckers.

The Fallen Nest

AFTER A terrible storm, I walked through our yard and picked up branches. Under a tall oak tree, I saw a tiny nest made from thin blades of grass. It was lined with long, stiff horsehair from Holly across the road and with soft fur from our dog Smokey, a husky. Inside the dog-hair lining were indentations where two little eggs had once rested.

Humbled, I realized I had unknowingly provided the bird parents with some of the building supplies for their home. We had planted and mowed the grass they had gathered and woven together. We had brushed our dog and let the wind carry the hair into the woods. The fragile abode had been blown about by the winds but was still intact.

We often make valuable contributions to the lives of others without even realizing it. A bag of clothes for victims of a disaster, a box of food to a homeless shelter, a word of encouragement to someone with a downcast expression are as a blade of grass in a field for many of us. Yet even small gifts can be pivotal in the life of someone needing strength to endure the storms they face in life.

Jesus said blessed are those who fed Him when He was hungry, gave Him a drink when He was thirsty and hospitality when He was a stranger. He said those who clothed Him, cared for Him when He was sick, and visited Him in prison would be given their inheritance that was prepared for them since the creation of the world. When asked, "Lord, when did we see you in these conditions so that we could do these things for you?" He explained, " 'Whatever you did for one of the least of these brothers of mine, you did for me' " (Matthew 25:40).

The little nest now sits in my hutch, reminding me of the promise in Ephesians 6:7–8 that whatever I do, if I will do it with my whole heart, as if I were serving the Lord, He will bless the fruit of my labor beyond my comprehension.

Bird Feeder:

God is able to do more than all we ask or imagine, according to His power that is at work within us (see Ephesians 3:20).

Birdbath:

" 'But when you give to the needy, do not let your left hand know what your right hand is doing, so that your giving may be in secret. Then your Father, who sees what is done in secret, will reward you' "(Matthew 6:3–4).

Birdhouse:

*I will not underestimate
what You are able to do
with a small beginning.*

For the Birds:

When robins and other ground feeders return early to frozen ground and little food, put out dog food, apple pieces, and raisins soaked in water to help them through until spring.

The Old
Oak Tree

THE TEMPERATURE dipped below zero, and my dogs needed to come in the house. I slipped on my boots and headed out. As the door slammed shut, I groaned—I was locked out. On our little country road, I was the only one home, and no extra keys lay hidden under any rocks. I climbed in my car, shivering and praying for a way into my house. Out in the cold again, I tried to break in without doing any damage, but nothing would budge. I headed back for the car to escape the bitter chill of the wind.

My teeth chattering, I prayed, asking the Lord for a blessing. I looked around the winter wonderland and noticed something moving on the oak tree next to the car. A bird with a curved bill blinked at me and went back to working on the rugged bark. A brown creeper! I had been hoping for a long time to see this little feathered creature. He looked at me again, then flew away. Seeing the bird was fun, but the cold was steadily creeping into my body. Something had to be done!

With no other choice, I headed for the basement door and did what the actors on TV do when they are in this situation—I bashed the door in with my foot. The heat inside the house washed over my cold face. I put on the teapot and thanked the Lord for our furnace. Bracing up the door, I smiled. God didn't miraculously unlock the door, but I did see an unexpected blessing on the bark of the oak.

He showed me that some answers are harder to find than others, but we need to keep "creeping" on in faith, even though our advancement seems imperceptible. God said we would find Him when we seek Him with our whole heart and soul (see Deuteronomy 4:29). I remembered the first place we are to look for Him is on the side of a tree on Calvary. No one expected a Savior to rescue us from a rugged cross. But God slowly reveals bits of His big plan for us one tiny step at a time. I whispered a prayer of thanksgiving and limped to the phone. My husband needed to know the door was damaged but all was well with my soul!

BIRD FEEDER:
Knock and keep on knocking, and the door will be opened to you.

BIRDBATH:
"And when they were come to the place, which is called Calvary, there they crucified him [Jesus], and the malefactors, one on the right hand, and the other on the left. Then said Jesus, 'Father, forgive them; for they know not what they do' " (Luke 23:33–34 KJV).

BIRDHOUSE:
"Those who know your name
will trust in you,
for you, LORD, have never forsaken
those who seek you."

PSALM 9:10

FOR THE BIRDS:

Birds especially need extra fat intake when the weather is cold. Keep suet in small hanging cages built to keep wild animals and neighboring dogs out of this rich snack.

The Swan

ONE WARM Sunday afternoon, my parents took my little brother and me to the lake. Clutched in our hands were bright polka-dot bread bags. We were going to feed the geese. I loved being surrounded by the big birds and had often watched them eat right out of my dad's hand. Today I was going to try it, too!

To my delight, the swans came to us first, and to my five-year-old body, they were huge. In the water, they were graceful and seemed lighter than air. But on land they waddled clumsily on black legs that seemed too skinny to hold up their big, white bodies. Dad offered the first bite of bread to a swan that gobbled it down.

I eagerly reached in the bag and grabbed a piece of bread. Tearing off a corner, I held it out for the swan, but I forgot to let go of it. The swan's mouth closed around my fingers and pulled. A short tug-of-war began. The swan eventually got the bread. I got hissed at and a sore finger. The skin wasn't broken, but my heart was shocked. Tears filled my eyes as my concerned parents checked me over. "But why did the swan bite me?" I asked, choking back my desire to cry.

In order for the swan and me to have a good relationship, I needed to let go of the bread. I had a gift that allowed me to stand in the presence of the swan. If I let go of the bread, I would lose my connection with the beautiful bird. But when I didn't, I got hurt. In the wonder of being the center of the swan's attention, I forgot my reason for being there in the first place. The swan became frustrated, and I felt confused.

We all have a gift in the palm of our hand that others are hungry to receive. God has gifted each of us with unique abilities for edifying and collaborating with others to make a better world. These natural talents are like the bag of bread that we didn't mix or bake. Without intensive studies, some of us can paint, care for children, sing, organize an office, or make things grow with amazing ease. These inborn skills that give us pleasure to perform are our "God-given gifts" that contribute to God's plan to meet people's needs.

But our own immaturity brings conflict when giving gifts because we tend to want recognition, gratitude, and even reward in return. We pray, "Lord, use me where I can share this gift You have given to me with others." Then, before long, we're whining, "Lord, they're just using me and they don't even thank me for what I do for them."

We sometimes hear, "Let go and let God." It is easy to say, yet hard to do. But to truly enjoy the gifts that God designed into the center of our purpose, we have to let go of what we have freely received and let God, alone, reward us.

BIRD FEEDER:

" 'Give, and it will be given to you. A good measure, pressed down, shaken together and running over, will be poured into your lap. For with the measure you use, it will be measured to you' " (Luke 6:38).

BIRDBATH:
"Each one should use whatever gift he has received to serve others, faithfully administering God's grace in its various forms. If anyone speaks, he should do it as one speaking the very words of God. If anyone serves, he should do it with the strength God provides, so that in all things God may be praised through Jesus Christ. To him be the glory and the power for ever and ever" (1 Peter 4:10–11).

BIRDHOUSE:
*Lord, give me the faith to
let go of childish attachments to my gifts.*

FOR THE BIRDS:
Keep a journal listing the birds you have seen. Record where you were, what they were doing, and what you were thinking at the time. Or simply mark your sightings on a calendar as you see new birds. Record significant birding dates

such as how often you buy seed, put up new houses, and see babies at the feeders. It's fun to read your calendar notes or journal on New Year's Eve.

The Thank-You Song

AS DUSK settled over the woods, the urgent call of a cardinal broke the silence. A male redbird fluttered at the kitchen window where I was drying the dishes. My husband and I went outside to see what was disturbing him. He flew just ahead of us, continuing his agitated cry. He landed near a female on a nest. It took a moment for our eyes to adjust to the twilight.

As we scanned the trees, we found the source of the bird's emergency. Almost invisible in the tree above the nest sat a huge owl. We watched for a while; then the owl blinked his yellow eyes, opened his wings, and glided silently away. We turned to go back in the house, amazed that the cardinal had led us to his home.

The redbird followed us to the house, where we stopped by the door. He sat in the brambles near us and sang to us again. This time the melody was lovely. Jon said, "It's as if he was saying thank you." We watched him rejoin his family in the nest.

I returned to the dishes and wondered if the cardinal knew we would help him. I marveled at the wonderful and mysterious ways of God. Like the cardinal, I sometimes need someone bigger to help me out of a desperate situation. When I do, God is quick to respond. He doesn't turn away to finish what He is doing in the rest of the universe. His attention is immediately drawn to my fluttering heart and urgent call for help.

Bird Feeder:

"Do not forsake your friend and the friend of your father, and do not go to your brother's house when disaster strikes you—better a neighbor nearby than a brother far away" (Proverbs 27:10).

BIRDBATH:

"If you make the Most High your dwelling. . . then no harm will befall you. . . . For he will command his angels concerning you to guard you in all your ways. . . . 'Because he loves me,' says the LORD, 'I will rescue him; I will protect him, for he acknowledges my name. He will call upon me, and I will answer him; I will be with him in trouble, I will deliver him and honor him. With long life will I satisfy him and show him my salvation' " (Psalm 91:9–11, 14–16).

BIRDHOUSE:

"I will take refuge in the shadow of your wings until the disaster has passed."

PSALM 57:1

FOR THE BIRDS:

If you own a cat that frequently stalks your feeders, or if the stalker is your neighbor's cat, ask them to consider putting a bell on the cat's collar to alert birds of this potential predator.

The Wedding Guest

GUESTS GATHERED in the woodland clearing and waited. Sunlight bathed the altar, and birds sang sweetly in the branches. Wedding music started, and we turned to watch for the bride.

From the back row, I watched in wonder as she walked the grassy aisle. Unbeknownst to her, an unexpected guest hovered behind her. Drawn by the color and fresh scent of the flowers in her hair, a male ruby-throated hummingbird joined the wedding party to escort the bride to her groom. His emerald and ruby feathers looked like an elegant tuxedo perfect for the occasion!

Her groom smiled at her, rejoicing in the sweetness of his bride as the iridescent guest hovered nearby with mutual attentiveness to her movements. We could see the groom's joy and read his thoughts through the expression on his face. "Isn't she beautiful?" his eyes boasted as he vowed to love her forever.

It was a sweet glimpse of the mysterious relationship God offers us through Jesus Christ. When we accept Jesus as Lord of our life, the Word of God likens our covenant with Christ as a marriage. He sends His Holy Spirit to us as a seal of our promise and makes it evident to the world that we belong to Him. Like the hummingbird at the wedding, the Holy Spirit hovers near us, drawing attention to what is good in us and giving radiance to our countenance.

One day Jesus will stand before the world with those who love Him and say, "Behold, I present my bride, my church, whom I love more than my own flesh. I nourished her, carefully protected her and cherished her, and now look at her glorious splendor" (see Ephesians 5:27). All those at the wedding ceremony will become a part of His sweet promise of eternal love.

Bird Feeder:
" 'Blessed are those who are invited to the wedding supper of the Lamb!' " (Revelation 19:9).

Birdbath:
"Surely goodness and love will follow me all the days of my life, and I will dwell in the house of the LORD forever" (Psalm 23:6).

Birdhouse:
Yes, Lord,
I choose to belong to You.

For the Birds:
Hummingbirds are mostly attracted to red, but don't use red food coloring in hummingbird water. The dyes can be harmful to them. Instead choose feeders with red or orange on them.

Turkey Buzzards

ONE SUMMER a family of turkey buzzards roosted single file on the peak of our roof. I was used to watching these large birds from afar. They gracefully circled the skies overhead in search of food. Our company would often mistake them for eagles, but a close view of them reveals that nothing could be further from the truth! Their red, featherless heads, slumped shoulders, and greasy, ratty feathers aren't beautiful. A friend of mine declared when he saw them, stating the obvious, "They are UG-ly birds!"

However, turkey buzzards are much more than what the eye beholds. While their circling just appears to be lazy circles, they are systematic hunters. Although their beaks and talons are not designed to attack live flesh, they do eat animals lost to road kill and natural death. They have the unique ability to kill any virus or bacteria they digest, and yet their own droppings are disease free. As cleanup crews, they fight the spread of infectious disease in our woods and on country roads.

They are dependable parents who stay with their young to teach them the ways of survival. They live in a communal roost, often in the same tree, perched on the same branch for most of their lives. They can venture two hundred miles in search of food, then return to their designated limb two weeks later. When a large meal is found, such as the carcass of a dead cow or deer, they somehow communicate to other roosts of vultures that live as far as thirty miles away to share their find and help with the cleanup.

These good neighbors are friendly to people, too, often choosing to live as close to humans as possible. Many have been known to befriend joggers and children walking to bus stops by showing up each day at their scheduled venue. Wounded birds in rehabilitation grow so attached to their caretaker, they follow them around like pet dogs. How unfortunate if we judge these intelligent and loving birds by their looks.

Without self-regard, turkey buzzards show themselves as friendly, serve their community, and thrive because they do it faithfully. Yet society often ignores or disregards the unattractive. The turkey vultures remind us, however, that beauty is a way of life and not just a visual attraction. Sometimes we have to look a little deeper to find the treasure hidden within all of God's creation.

BIRD FEEDER:

" 'Blessed [happy, to be envied, and spiritually prosperous—with life-joy and satisfaction in God's favor and salvation, regardless of their outward conditions] are the poor in spirit [the humble, who rate themselves insignificant], for theirs is the kingdom of heaven' " (Matthew 5:3).

BIRDBATH:

" 'The LORD does not look at the things man looks at. Man looks at the outward appearance, but the LORD looks at the heart' " (1 Samuel 16:7).

BIRDHOUSE:

Create in me a pure heart, O God,
and renew a willingness within me
to share what I have with others.

SEE PSALM 51:10, 12

FOR THE BIRDS:

Sparrows are often disregarded by beginning birders. But this family of birds displays a wonderful variety of markings. Study the field guides, and then watch closely for the subtle differences in these friendly birds. Millet or thistle on the ground will attract the song sparrow, the house sparrow, Harris's sparrow, the white-crowned, the golden-crowned, and the white-throated sparrow. There are many more to be enjoyed and added to your life-list journal of birds.

Woody

I THOUGHT Woody the Woodpecker was an exaggerated, make-believe character, so I was surprised the first time I saw the large, red-crested bird on our oak tree. The bird was obviously a woodpecker, but he was the size of a crow or bigger. His powerful moves against the tree sounded like hammering. Wood chips flew in all directions. He paused, cocked his head, and moved up the tree, where he attacked a new spot.

I reached for my bird book. There he was— a pileated woodpecker. I continued to watch him. The bird reminded me of the ptero-dactyls in *The Flintstones;* he was clumsy and prehistoric-looking. Bugs under the bark didn't stand a chance against him. He worked the tree, moving only when he exterminated the insects in the hole he had made. I heard a loud vibrato call in the woods; he raised his head, answered, and flew away.

In studying more about the bird, I learned woodpeckers help trees survive the invasion of destructive insects. They pound out bugs in the tree bark that would otherwise rob the trees of life-giving sap. Within a few days, the wounds left on the tree from the woodpecker's search for food are covered with a healing, white substance, protecting the tree from further damage.

We can sometimes feel like the oak tree bugged by invading forces. In spite of faith to shield us from outside circumstances, painful experiences somehow worm their way into our memories, infecting our optimism and our hope of the future. These external moments of failure, insults, or disappointments can burrow deep into our hearts before we even realize they have attached themselves to us.

These attachments need to be hammered out, yet we feel defenseless against these intruders. If these life-draining inner conflicts are not removed, we suffer from ungodly pain deep within our hearts. But God sends woodpeckers to save the trees and the truth of His Word to save us.

If we simply ask God for deliverance, His

Holy Spirit will search out the things that beset our joy like the tenacious woodpecker searching for worms beneath the bark of a tree. He won't move on until we are cleansed by His loving attention.

Once made clean by God's Spirit, peace, patience, kindness, goodness, and gentleness will energize our lives again (see Galatians 5:22–23). As the trees once marred by the woodpecker's probing, we, too, will heal without a trace of the surgery performed by the Holy Spirit's refining touch.

BIRD FEEDER:

"For you, O God, tested us; you refined us like silver" (Psalm 66:10).

BIRDBATH:

"For the word of God is living and active. Sharper than any double-edged sword, it penetrates even to dividing soul and spirit, joints and marrow; it judges the thoughts and attitudes of the heart. Nothing in all creation is hidden from God's sight. . . . Let us then approach the throne of grace with confidence, so that we may receive mercy and find grace to help us in our time of need" (Hebrews 4:12–13, 16).

BIRDHOUSE:

Lord, I will consider it all joy when
I encounter various trials,
knowing that the testing
of my faith produces endurance.
I will let endurance have its perfect result,
that I may be perfected and completed,
lacking in nothing (see James 1:2–4).
I trust You, Lord,
knowing You care for the birds,
and You care much more for me.

FOR THE BIRDS:

If you have a dead tree nearby that is not where it could cause damage if it fell, keep it. Let it be a reminder of how we felt before we understood God's love for us. Woodpeckers, flickers, nuthatches, brown creepers, and chickadees will work the tree and entertain the bird-watchers at your house.

Additional Reading

Books

Harrison, Hal H. Peterson Field Guides, *Birds' Nests.* Boston, MA: Houghton Mifflin Company, 1975.

Kress, Stephen W. National Audubon Society, *The Bird Garden—A comprehensive guide to attracting birds to your backyard throughout the year.* New York: DK Publishing, Inc., 1995.

Peterson, Roger Tory. Peterson Field Guides, *A Field Guide to Birds of Eastern and Central North America.* Boston, MA: Houghton Mifflin Company, 1980.

Stokes, Donald W., and Lillian Q. Stokes Nature Guides, *A Guide to Bird Behavior, Vol. 1.* Boston and Toronto: Little, Brown and Company, 1979.

Stokes, Donald W., and Lillian Q. Stokes Nature Guides, *A Guide to Bird Behavior, Vol. 2.* Boston and Toronto: Little, Brown and Company, 1983.

Stokes, Donald W., and Lillian Q. Stokes Nature Guides, *A Guide to Bird Behavior, Vol. 3.* Boston and Toronto: Little, Brown and Company, 1989.

MAGAZINES

Audubon. To subscribe: 1-800-274-4201. For information on how to become a member of the National Audubon Society, write to: Membership Dept., 700 Broadway, New York, NY 10003. Telephone (212) 979-3000.

Birder's World is a great magazine to keep bird-watchers informed of favorite foods, houses, and popular hangouts for various birds. Write to: Birder's World, P.O. Box 1612, Waukesha, WI 53187-9950, or call 1-800-533-6644.

Birds & Blooms is another colorful magazine (with no advertising) for bird enthusiasts. Write to: Birds & Blooms, P.O. Box 984, Greendale, WI 52129 to subscribe.

FAVORITE WEB SITES

www.birdersworld.com

www.stokesbirdsathome.com: for great birding tips and TV series' updates.

www.wingsbirds.com: for bird-watching tours in sixty countries on seven continents. Telephone (520) 320-9368.

ABOUT THE AUTHORS

CRISTINE BOLLEY is the series editor for this line of special-interest devotionals from Barbour Publishing, Inc. Her mission is to explain, exemplify, and establish the truth of God's power and the grace of His love with clarity. Through writing books and speaking at motivational conferences, she inspires people to trust God for His purpose, plan, provision, and power to enjoy the abundant life His Good News proclaims. Being well traveled and having served in missions while living in Mexico and New Zealand, Cristine feels a passion for the global task of reaching people with the Gospel of Jesus Christ.

Cristine and James (her best friend and husband) enjoy time with their three daughters, Jamie, Erin, and Lindsey, their son-in-law, Will, and their new granddaughter, Riley. When not writing or watching her daughters play volleyball, Cristine enjoys having tea with friends, making scrapbooks, or browsing antique stores. Bird-watching, however, has been a year-round, lifetime hobby shared by both her immediate and extended family.

In the last few years, Cristine has authored,

ghostwritten, or co-authored fifteen books and always has two or three works in progress. Her first illustrated book for children was released in the fall of 2001, titled *A Gift from St. Nicholas*. She co-authored *What I Learned from God while Quilting* and *What I Learned from God while Gardening*, both released by Promise Press, an imprint of Barbour Publishing, Inc.

Contact Cristine Bolley at:
Wings Unlimited
P.O. Box 691532
Tulsa, OK 74169–1532

JOY DEKOK lives in Rochester, Minnesota, with her husband, Jon, and their dog Bandit. Since childhood, she has enjoyed feeding, watching, and learning about birds. She continues to write about the birds she sees and is also working on a novel.

Joy looks forward to her time with family and friends, Bible study, reading, and walking. One of her favorite walking spots in her area is around Silver Lake, where thousands of wintering Canada geese reside during the cooler months. Some make the lake their permanent home, so Joy is able to feed them and watch their young grow.

The DeKoks attend Calvary Evangelical Free Church. Joy inspires others as she speaks to groups on the topics of birds, journal keeping, and wild-flower gardening. She is collecting stories for a sequel, *What Else God Taught Us while Watching Birds.* You are invited to share your bird stories with her by writing to the following address.

Contact Joy E. DeKok at:
P.O. Box 6285
Rochester, MN 55903

Inspirational Library

Beautiful purse/pocket-size editions of Christian classics bound in flexible leatherette. These books make thoughtful gifts for everyone on your list, including yourself!

When I'm on My Knees   The highly popular collection of devotional thoughts on prayer, especially for women.
    Flexible Leatherette $4.97

The Bible Promise Book   Over 1,000 promises from God's Word arranged by topic. What does God promise about matters like: Anger, Illness, Jealousy, Love, Money, Old Age, and Mercy? Find out in this book!
    Flexible Leatherette $3.97

Daily Wisdom for Women   A daily devotional for women seeking biblical wisdom to apply to their lives. Scripture taken from the New American Standard Version of the Bible.
    Flexible Leatherette $4.97

My Daily Prayer Journal   Each page is dated and features a Scripture verse and ample room for you to record your thoughts, prayers, and praises. One page for each day of the year.
    Flexible Leatherette $4.97

Available wherever books are sold.
Or order from:

Barbour Publishing, Inc.
P.O. Box 719
Uhrichsville, OH 44683
http://www.barbourbooks.com

If you order by mail, add $2.00 to your order for shipping.
Prices are subject to change without notice.